Help others grow.

Lauren

HELP
Others
GROW
FIRST

Help others grow.
Simon

Advance Praise for *Help Others Grow First*

"The book is amazing, as always. It truly depicts the daily struggles to attract and maintain qualified employees and to grow their workforce in a manner that provides stability and growth opportunities. We are in unchartered territory with today's workforce. This book provides fundamental and practical information to help employers provide the culture all employees want to work for. In a day and age where information comes at us from all directions, it is easy to get distracted from what is really important, our staff. Our staff is what builds our business and creates the success stories we all hope to achieve when we manage people. Through the book, I can identify things I need to work on as a manager and leader within my organization to make our workplace better, building the people who choose to work for and with me to be the best possible place to work. Thank you, Lauren, for time and time again sharing your fun, unique, and educational perspectives on a variety of topics to help us build better teams, lead people, and improve the cultures of our organizations one step at a time!"

Matt Crouse, Director of Parks and Recreation, City of Nixa, MO

"Retaining and engaging exceptional talent is the nerve center of leaders charged with scaling companies in these uncertain times. Lauren Schieffer challenges the reader to look in a mirror as the first step in attracting great talent. Mastering the nine principles she chronicles is at the nerve center of building a culture that will attract A players. Today the best talent has options to choose from. Lauren's guideposts will lead you to becoming the recruiting magnet that attracts a team cable of raising the bar on expected results."

Mike Lejeune, President, Lighting the Path

"This book is a clear and well-thought-out manifesto on what leadership *should* look like. Lauren's *Nine Essentials* offer a straightforward path to attracting the best employees and then keeping them. Every leader can benefit from the concept of helping others grow first."

Dr. Nido Qubein, President, High Point University

"Lauren Schieffer has done it again! In her 4th book, *Help Others Grow First*, Lauren takes us along a rolling journey of significant leadership – with nine stops along the way. Each stop is as rich, insightful, and enjoyable as the last and the next, and each one brings us to a new depth in understanding how to find and keep our best people, our best leaders, at every phase of growth and success. Lauren tells her story and shares the stories of many others along this journey in her own genuine and lovely voice. She is a master of language, image, metaphor, and vision while engaging us on every page to ride along and learn!"

Roxanne M. Kaufman, President & CEO, ProLaureate Ltd.

"In *Help Others Grow First*, Lauren Schieffer challenges the traditional hierarchical mentality that treats employees as replaceable commodities and offers a new way of thinking about leadership that puts people at the center of the equation.

Dr. Robyn Odegaard, Mental MacGyver,
author, *Creating Success Out of Chaos*

"Unexpected employee turnover is very expensive and can destroy a company's culture. Lauren Schieffer's new book provides leaders a roadmap to dramatically reduce this problem, which is great for a company's bottom line and employee morale. If you are a leader that believes leadership should be rewarding and not difficult, do yourself a favor and infuse the author's Nine Essentials of Significant Leadership into your company's DNA. You'll be glad you did!"

"With her insightful and practical advice, Schieffer offers a roadmap to creating a workplace culture where employees feel valued and supported and where their growth and development are the top priority. She argues that leaders who prioritize the growth of their team members are more likely to attract and retain top talent and create a high-performance organization that achieves its goals."

Earl Bell, author, *Winning in Baseball and Business – Transforming Little League Principles into Major League Profits for Your Company*

"This is a must read for all leaders. Today's environment for growing great companies and retaining great employees has changed significantly from what it was in years past. Employees are looking for something different, a deeper motivation. In *Help Others Grow First*, Lauren reveals what it takes to make a company great by making great leaders. It is an experience of honest self-evaluation and a look at how we are seen by and affect others under our leadership. It is not only about personal development. It is about developing others around us to move them forward in our organizations. Through her *Nine Essentials of Significant Leadership*, Lauren offers the tools needed to develop into a great leader who develops great employees. This is an easy read and packed with inspiration, insight, and methods of practical application."

Carolyn Hanna, General Manager, Gary's Plumbing and Heating

"This new book, *Help Others Grow First*, will help anyone assess themselves and how they lead others. It is a concise, insightful, and necessary reminder of how we should all approach leadership, mentorship, and relationship, whether it is in business or our personal day-to-day lives. Lauren is a voice in this confusion of our world that embodies compassion and skills that are so needed. This is an easy but important read if you want to move to the next level of leadership or if you want to build a significant team of workers."

Robin Gandin, Owner, The SOULutionist, SOULcial Wellness

"In *Help Others Grow First*, Lauren Schieffer explains the complex subject of leadership in a way that anyone can understand and implement. In the post-Covid era of scarcity not only of qualified and motivated team members but also of meaningful and fulfilling jobs, this book is a must-read for employers and employees alike. And the added bonus is that Lauren's nine principles are universally applicable to all aspects of life. Living by the wisdom inspired by Lauren's Dad, The Colonel, will bring about a richer, more rewarding life for anyone who's breathing!

I will use this book as a teaching tool in all my coaching endeavors. It is THAT good!"

Alan G Stern, DDS, Dental Practitioner, speaker, author, and founder and lead coach, Better, Richer, Stronger, LLC

"Everyone is asking, 'How do we acquire and retain great employees?' Whether you are a new or experienced leader, Lauren Schieffer reminds us of the importance of using the 'power within' our own personal characteristics to become an effective and inspirational leader that others will aspire to follow. She outlines the concepts in an easily comprehendible format. It may sound simple, but Lauren emphasizes the importance of challenging ourselves to become better leaders through our daily interactions and recognizing the significance of helping others to become the best they can be by simply treating them with respect and understanding and acknowledging their presence and contributions. She offers various concepts that can be initiated by any leader who is passionate about becoming a truly impactful and motivating leader that everyone wishes to work for in a thriving world."

Paula McLain, Human Resources, Northwest Missouri State University

"Lauren's ability to share practical leadership tips based on real-world knowledge, experience, and data shines forth again. Any leader who reads *Help Others Grow First* will come away with strategies to assist in the recruitment and retention of top talent – even in the new workforce landscape we find ourselves."

Susan Wathen, Vice President, Human Resources, Hannibal Regional Healthcare System

"This is a must-read for all leaders in business as well as volunteer organizations. Lauren's thoughts are timely and relevant in today's environment when we have a choice more than ever about our work and volunteer life. As a member and regional leader from Rotary International, this resonates with our Four Way Test of all the things we think, say, and do. As a financial professional, it reminds me that how we make people 'feel' is very important. The way we were treated as up-and-coming leaders wasn't always done with love and respect. As leaders today, we need to do better and lead by example with integrity and respect always. Thank you, Lauren, for these important tools, techniques, and reminders to help make the world a better place for all."

Jill Pietrusinski, Int'l Assembly Training Leader, Rotary International

"This is not a management book. It is a leadership book! Whether you are a business owner, department head, pastor, teacher, parent, you are a leader and would benefit from Lauren's expertise in the elements of leadership. We've all seen leaders who try to 'lighten up' a meeting with a joke about a staff member or rebuff questions or feedback. Leaders would do well to bookmark Essential #6 Communicate Respectfully."

Judy Bond, President, The Bond Team

"We lead others when we first lead ourselves and that is exactly what this book helps you do. It's packed with stories that bring the insights to life. This book is a difference-maker because Lauren knows that leadership begins within. You'll finish the book being a better person and, in turn, a better leader."

Mark Hunter, "The Sales Hunter," author of *A Mind for Sales*

"Whether you are a new leader or a seasoned leader, *Help Others Grow First* is a must-read if you want to step up your game to become a significant leader. Lauren Schieffer breaks down her Nine Essentials of Significant Leaders (which includes vision, integrity, humility, empathy, and accountability, to name a few) and provides a vision of a company everyone should want to work for where her nine essentials are actively practiced. Combined with clear and practical insights, leaders of every level can certainly use this book as a roadmap for growth and excellent corporate culture."

Whitney Kelso, Elevance Health

"Lauren's unique ability to perform the research coupled with her derived knowledge, which allows her to speak at all corporate levels, has raised the adeptness of HR with growing and developing future employees."

Mike Polis, Vice President of Human Resources, Jay R. Smith Mfg. Co., Division of Morris Group International

"How do you measure a good leader? By noticing how little their workers need them and how much they want them around anyway. Your job as a leader is to become progressively less necessary to the daily operations. That allows you to focus on bigger issues while your team does the essential work. But if you don't make an honest effort to care for and care about your people, you soon won't have any 'people.' Helping people grow has been my company motto since the 1970s, and it warms my heart to see Lauren Schieffer is carrying the same torch into the future. Grow your people first!"

Jim Cathcart, author of *Mentor Minutes*, Top 1% TEDx speaker, Sales & Marketing Hall of Fame

How Smart Leaders
Attract & Retain Great Employees

Lauren Ann Schieffer

HELP *Others* GROW FIRST

How Smart Leaders Attract & Retain Great Employees

© 2023 Lauren Ann Schieffer, CSP

All rights reserved. No part of this publication may be reproduced, distributed or transmitted in any form or by any means, including photocopying, recording, or other electronic or mechanical methods, without the prior written permission of the publisher, except in the case of brief quotations embodied in critical reviews and certain other noncommercial uses permitted by copyright law.

For permission requests, write to the publisher, addressed "Attention: Permissions Coordinator," at the address below.

>Lauren Schieffer, CSP/LSE Publications
>16125 152nd Street,
>Bonner Springs, KS

www.LaurenSchieffer.com

Bulk Ordering Information: LS@laurenschieffer.com

Quantity sales. Special discounts are available on quantity purchases by corporations, associations, and others. For details, contact the "Special Sales Department" at the email address above.

ISBN 979-8-218-15149-2

Cover & Interior Design by:
Melissa Farr, melissa@backporchcreative.com

Contents

Part I   The New Struggle to Attract and Retain Great Employees 1
    Why You are Losing Your Best People 5
    How to Solve the Revolving Door Dilemma 9

Part II   The Nine Essentials of Significant Leadership 17
    Essential #1 – Understand Your Own Value 21
    Essential #2 – Treat All People with Respect 29
    Essential #3 – Act with Integrity at All Times 37
    Essential #4 – Open Your Mind to New Possibilities 45
    Essential #5 – Craft a Vision 51
    Essential #6 – Communicate Respectfully 57
    Essential #7 – Lead by Example 65
    Essential #8 – Celebrate the Results of Others 71
    Essential #9 – Work for Your Replacement 77

Part III   Going Forward into the Future 83
    Why Good People Stay – Living the Nine Essentials 85
    A Final Thought 99

Acknowledgments *103*
About the Author *105*
Can Hiring Lauren Benefit You? *106*
Works Cited *107*

PART I

The New Struggle to Attract and Retain Great Employees

In the new reality of a post-COVID-19 world, the number one concern facing C-level executives is attracting and retaining great employees to fulfill their corporate vision and strategy. To most, it feels like an uphill battle, as the workforce is looking at this new reality from a completely different perspective and leaving their jobs in numbers not seen in recent memory. The so-called "Great Resignation" has continued, even as other aspects of life return to some semblance of pre-pandemic normalcy. In a 2022 global worker survey from Microsoft, 41 percent of workers surveyed were considering resigning or changing careers. Research shows a record 47.4 million workers actually took the leap and quit their jobs in 2021.[1] These numbers are significant, but they don't tell the whole story. They don't help us understand why companies are losing their best people.

The revolving door dilemma, often called churn, is real; however, this dilemma does not have to be your new permanent reality. It is possible to attract, retain, energize, and grow top-notch employees regardless of external economic or cultural conditions. How can employers make this happen? In order to block this revolving door, we have to *help others grow first* using the concept of significant leadership. In the following chapters, I will delve into what significant leadership means and give an in-depth look at The Nine Essentials of Significant Leadership. But, in order to begin, we must first ask this important question: Why do good people leave?

Why You Are Losing Your Best People

As we head further into the 21st century, the need for significant leadership has never been more acute. The generic, efficiency-leadership model of the 20th century will not guide companies, the nation, or the world out of their current plight because, to a considerable extent, efficiency leadership is what led to the situation in the first place. Efficiency leadership is only one fractional step above management. It focuses on the accumulation of wealth, profit, accolades, market share, lean success, productivity, and achieving more with less. While there is nothing inherently wrong with any of these objectives at a surface level, when any of them becomes the focal point to the detriment of the workforce, it can become much more destructive than productive. Exit interviews that I have conducted for my clients over the past two years have made this very clear. (These are true stories, but the names have been changed.)

Suzie, a top salesperson for a healthcare software firm, said, "I'm tired of being treated like a commodity. I am not a commodity. I'm a human being, and the travel schedule they expect me to maintain is not sustainable. I am not a robot."

Rob, a call center manager, shared, "I get that we need to make our numbers. They keep telling us we need to make the numbers. But the numbers are not realistic. Who came up with them anyway? No one ever asked me if my team is even physically capable of making those kinds of numbers. Everyone is at critical burnout already. They keep pushing for more without giving me any reason why I should push my team for more or how it matters to them."

Pat, a tenured project manager for a national laboratory, cited the lack of transparency, the secrets, and the poor communication from the top down, which created a culture of insecurity and uncertainty that was no longer tolerable.

Contrary to what traditionalists and curmudgeons may say, the mass exodus following the pandemic is not because people are generally lazy. It's not because ongoing pandemic assistance programs incentivized people not to work. It's because we have entered a new world regarding office environments, and people are discovering what they really want from their work. Although uncertain times and lingering trauma from the pandemic may have forced everyone to rethink their priorities in life and work, make no mistake – this shift has been coming for a long time. The pandemic merely forced it through a wormhole into our laps sooner than expected. What was previously a slow simmer ignited into a rolling boil of discontent seemingly overnight.

No one enjoys working at a job where they dread coming to work or are just getting by with the minimum effort to get a paycheck.

While in the past such employees might have stuck it out in a toxic working environment indefinitely, the pandemic opened cracks in the opportunity wall. This means that companies coasting along with a pre-pandemic culture, assuming it's still adequate or beneficial without reassessing their employee experience, are in for a rude awakening (if it hasn't happened already). Such head-in-the-sand thinking inevitably leads to high turnover, worker apathy, unhappy clients, and decreased revenue.

The substantial attrition numbers seen post-pandemic do not mean that these masses of people all decided to stay home, sitting on their backsides, watching reality TV, and eating cheese puffs. No, most of them found something better suited to their needs, or they started their own businesses and may soon be your competitors. Granted, many baby boomers did take the opportunity to reassess their retirement plans, deciding that now was the time. This is not, however, the primary factor at play here. The "great resignation" is really the intense concentration – the culmination, if you will – of a process that has been brewing for quite a while, as the youngest two generations in America become the prevailing force in the workplace. The pandemic simply crystallized and solidified their need to work and be productive on their own terms.

As was made very clear in those exit interviews, the primary reason people leave their jobs is because of a toxic company culture that values production over people and sees employees as disposable or replaceable. When Sami (again, name changed for privacy), a contract corporate trainer, asked to renegotiate her contract commensurate with the amount of income she brought to the company, she was told that one hundred trainers were waiting in the wings for the juicy engagements she was given. So, she decided to give those other trainers the opportunity and canceled her contract.

I also heard former employees communicate over and over again about the lack of a healthy work-life balance, poor leadership, no flexibility about working from home, and unclear relevance. While this revolving door syndrome continues, a leader's attention will be consistently distracted by filling positions and finding the right people to do the work, which pulls them away from crafting a vision, growing the people on their team, and achieving the vision of the organization. Therefore, it would behoove all employers, especially those that prioritize profits over employee wellbeing, to understand the link between leadership, corporate culture, and employee retention if they want to stay competitive and thrive.

How to Survive the Revolving Door Dilemma

The 20th-century standard of working for the same company for thirty years, becoming vested in your company's retirement plan, and then retiring with a gold watch and a hearty handshake has not been the reality for some time. And while many choose to attribute this to the millennial generation always looking for a better opportunity, the shift actually started on Wall Street and in the board rooms of America.

With the leveraged buyout mania of the 1980s, big companies gobbled up smaller ones, dissected them, and sold the pieces off for scraps. Loyalty to a company that is not loyal to you stopped making sense long before the newest generations joined the workforce.

One of my clients, "Justin," worked for three different companies over the course of five years without ever leaving his desk. When the company announced the last round of layoffs, he decided to move on, saying, "I don't want to be the last one here turning off the lights as the door hits me in the butt on my way out." When you add the roving nature of a younger workforce and everyone trying to make sense of a post-pandemic work environment, you have a prime breeding ground for the current revolving door syndrome.

So how do we break this cycle? We do it by creating a working environment grounded in loyalty to the employees. The majority of today's workforce has never been employed by a company that views them as their most valuable asset. Just as respect must be given before it is received, you can only establish loyalty in your workforce by being loyal to them first. This reciprocity is most effectively achieved through a focus on significant leadership.

Significant leadership shifts the focus from building numbers to building people, genuinely seeing and valuing every member of an organization for who they are and what they bring to the table. Based on the foundation of servant leadership, significant leadership seeks to create a legacy of strength in diversity, power in compassion, resilience in empathy, and results from accountability. Diversity is essential to a functioning society. Significant leaders strive to build engaged and empowered employees for a more universally inclusive generation of new leaders who are prepared to address global community issues in the future. Significant leadership allows not only for diversity but also for inclusion and equity, which creates a sense of belonging and, therefore, a more substantial buy-in to the organization's purpose, mission, and vision. Significant leaders can build a company culture that breeds loyalty, empowering employees and allowing them to grow to their desired potential on their own terms.

The Nine Essentials of Significant Leadership provide a format for achieving this. Although many skills are involved in developing leadership, nine essential concepts are absolutely required for *significant* leadership. While we will examine each of these in-depth in part two, I would like to briefly examine them here as we conclude this discussion of the revolving door dilemma.

The Nine Essentials of Significant Leadership

#1 – Understand your own value

Most arrogant, bombastic people I have met actually have minimal self-esteem and utilize arrogance as a defense mechanism. Having a solid sense of your own value as a human being gives you a foundation for humility, which is an essential quality of significant leadership.

#2 – Treat all people with respect

I have yet to meet anyone who is enthusiastic about working with or for someone who is disrespectful to them. Understanding the difference between respect for someone and respect to someone is crucial for significant leadership.

#3 – Act with integrity at all times

Your integrity defines your character, which helps establish your credibility as a leader. A team will only follow a leader whose integrity they can trust.

#4 – Open your mind to new possibilities

A closed mind cannot grow, and a closed mind cannot lead. Significant leadership looks at any situation from all directions and considers all possible solutions to a problem, even if they are different than expected.

#5 – Craft a vision

While crafting a vision may be Leadership 101 material, significant leaders build a vision that has a unique role for every member of their team to play. Therefore, the vision is not about the leader or the company but about the employees.

#6 – Communicate respectfully
While some people lean toward the passive side of the communication spectrum and others lean toward the aggressive, assertive communication is generally considered optimal. Significant leaders, however, go a step beyond assertive communication to respectful communication.

#7 – Lead by example
Leading by example is often discussed (ad nauseum!) but less often practiced to its fullest extent. Leading by example goes beyond what happens from 9:00am–5:00pm in the workplace.

#8 – Celebrate the results of others
Significant leaders are constantly looking for ways, large and small, to recognize the efforts and results of their team. Choosing significant leadership involves deciding to set aside personal recognition in favor of team recognition.

#9 – Work for your replacement
A leader's primary job is to replace themselves. The objectives that should drive significant leaders is always to help others grow and build a more extensive network of significant leaders.

The Star to Guide You
So, let this be the mantra that consistently supports your leadership: **help others grow first**. This means we focus on others' needs before our own. We help them determine and act upon whatever will get them to the next leadership level. We always put our recognition, desires, or needs on a backburner long enough to give others a leg

up first. Significant leadership focuses on service before self and making a positive impact on those you are leading. In addition, significant leaders help emerging leaders, who will eventually replace them, build their legacy, and carry the concepts of significance into the future. In fact, you will know you are a significant leader when people who talk about you don't talk about what you've achieved for yourself but rather what you've accomplished for the benefit of others. When that is the filter through which we view all our efforts, we become significant leaders.

My Road Toward Significant Leadership
Before you take a guided tour of the Nine Essentials, you should know something about your tour guide.

I am The Colonel's Daughter – in every sense of the term. It is so much more than a brand. It's who I am, physically, emotionally, and intellectually.

My father was a Lt. Colonel in the United States Air Force. He stood six feet, six and a half inches tall, and he was 285 pounds lean. Dad also had a personality that entered a room five minutes before he did. The Colonel was an all-around handyman, a mister-fix-it – truly the MacGyver of his day.

He was always working on or tinkering with something. He would work around the house. He'd work on our cars. He'd work on the neighbors' cars, and I would "help" him. "Helping" him usually involved sitting with him to keep him company and handing him a tool every now and then. I spent so many hours of my childhood sitting at his feet as he talked to me about life.

So many times, as he was imparting wisdom, he would stop in the middle of his thought and say, "Pay attention, kid. This is a road sign in your life. You need to decide if you're gonna follow it or not."

It wasn't until after he died that I realized what he was really talking about. The Road Signs were life lessons that he tried so hard to instill in me. They were guideposts he knew would be critical to my health, my happiness, and my positive impact on the world.

Nowadays, I call these guideposts "Colonels of Wisdom."

Every day, in one way or another, Dad challenged me to be significant. Most people are programmed to chase success. Success is inwardly focused. Success is about titles and paychecks, accomplishments, awards, and accolades. Success is all about "me." Significance, on the other hand, is outwardly focused. Significance is about being of service and making the world we touch a better place because we were here. It has nothing whatsoever to do with how much money you make, what your title is, how much perceived power you might have, or what your accolades might be. It's not about compensation packages or parking spots. Significance is entirely about how many lives you touch and how you choose to impact those lives – because how you impact others is a choice. Significance is about "we."

Dad often said, "Anyone can be successful, kiddo – making money, climbing the corporate ladder . . . that's easy. Choose to be significant." It is this Road Sign, this Colonel of Wisdom, that has become an integral part of my life's work.

Because of who my dad was and what he did for the Air Force, I've had the privilege of sitting at the feet of and learning from some genuinely significant leaders, in addition to The Colonel.

When we were stationed at Wright Patterson AFB in Dayton, Ohio, I had the opportunity to visit my father at his office on base. Dad was the Division Chief for the Flight Dynamics Laboratory, and they were doing secured visitor tours of certain areas of the laboratory. While I was there, Dad introduced me to (then) Lt. Colonel Colin Powell, who was visiting on a cross-branch assignment for the National War College. I was in middle school and just a little intimidated as I sat between my dad and Col. Powell during lunch. He was so nice and spoke to me like an adult, showing interest in my conversation and what I was passionate about at the time. I was certain that he and I would be fast friends for life. Of course, I was never in the presence of that great man again, but I followed his career very closely – everything he did and wrote – and learned everything I could from his example.

In college, I had the privilege of knowing and learning from the late John McCain, having worked on his first campaign for US Representative for District 1 in Arizona.

In my adult life, I have had the opportunity to know and learn from John C. Maxwell (the foremost global authority on servant leadership) and the late Mary Kay Ash, having been a sales director for Mary Kay Cosmetics for eleven years.

I've learned from each of these significant leaders, plus many others, and absorbed bits and pieces of what I believe, teach, and espouse from each of them. Over the past few years, I have condensed the most imperative of those concepts into the Nine Essentials that are the subject of this book. At a forty-thousand-foot level, these are the most crucial characteristics of significant leaders. So, let's look at each of them in more depth.

PART II

The Nine Essentials of Significant Leadership

So, if our objective is to slow down the revolving door (please note, I don't think it's realistic to believe it can be closed completely; there will always be a bit of churn), the most important question to ask ourselves is not, "Why do good people leave?" as we have done thus far, but rather, "Why do good people stay?"

According to a survey done jointly by Paychex and Executive Networks[2], overall job stability, performing meaningful work, and feeling valued as a member of the team were cited as the most important reasons employees continue to stay at their companies. My experience has proven that to be true. People stay committed to a company or organization when they genuinely care about the purpose and mission of the company, and they feel they are making a difference with their work. This is amplified when an employee feels the company is as committed to them as they are to the company. People stay when they feel seen as human beings, when they feel their efforts are appreciated, when they feel valued and challenged. People will be loyal to a company when the lines of communication are clear and flow both ways, when they are empowered to make their own decisions based on a clear understanding of the overall vision, when they feel recognized, and when they believe they have a clear path for growth in the organization.

If you want your employees to have this experience under your leadership, The Nine Essentials is the place to begin. We will start with Essential #1 – Understand Your Own Value.

ESSENTIAL #1

Understand Your Own Value

Significant leaders have a solid knowledge of their own value. They understand that they, like every human being on the planet, are worthy of merit simply because they exist. Human value is not determined by a person's parentage, their country of origin, who they're married to or dating, what their title or position is, how much money they have or make, what their abilities or disabilities might be, what size they wear, what color their skin, hair or eyes are – or any other external factor society might use to place value on a person. Every person's value rests simply in the fact that they exist. That value doesn't have to be earned, and it cannot be purchased. It just is.

There is a difference between self-confidence and self-esteem. Self-confidence tells you that you can perform a task well. It assures you that you are capable. *Self-esteem*, on the other hand, assures you that you have value. Self-esteem tells you that your worth does not rest in external factors or traditional measures of success. None of the things that society utilizes to assign value matter at all. You have healthy self-esteem when you know and believe that your value comes solely from your existence as a person.

Some people have that inherent value reinforced by their parents. They are the lucky ones, and I have the privilege of knowing a few of them. Their solid self-esteem allows them to release what anyone says about them, thinks about them, or does to them because they are *secure* in their own value. What I find especially impressive about those who have this self-esteem is that it frees them to be humble.

I've found that arrogance is really a sign of *low* self-esteem. I believe that if you crack open the inner core of most pushy, belligerent, arrogant people, you will find a very small child with no self-esteem. They have just protected themselves with layers of arrogance they have put on like a coat.

Although I've held many jobs in my life, my current vocation as a leadership consultant, keynote speaker, and trainer offers me the opportunity to travel all over the globe and meet all kinds of people. I have counseled leaders and managers with varying degrees of self-esteem.

One particular manager made a belabored point of instructing participants in team meetings to turn their cell phones off. Not on vibrate, because she could still hear it – no, she wanted them *off*. She expressed that texting under the table was also unacceptable because she could see that we were doing it, which was distracting to her. Whenever there was any sidebar chatter, as there often is in team meetings, she stopped altogether and glared at the participants until they stopped talking. Or, worse yet, she called them out on the chatter verbally. This manager was what many people might call brassy and aggressive in her behavior and consistently tried to impress upon her team that she would not take "anything from anyone." As a result, she constantly dealt with attrition and HR issues because employees were offended at being treated like preschoolers.

On another occasion, I was brought in to mediate drama between two peer managers at a different organization. One was terrific with the team members, always funny and upbeat. The other manager, however, was exceptionally passive-aggressive and consistently sent verbal and emotional "zingers" to undermine the other's credibility with the team. She veiled criticism and emotional abuse in the drippy sweet guise of "constructive input." Eventually, her behavior took a considerable toll on the other manager's confidence, productivity, and serenity, in addition to eroding both managers' credibility with the team.

When I look back at each of these situations empathetically, I believe that their behaviors resulted from low self-esteem. I imagine the first has a fear of being taken advantage of and not being taken seriously. Maybe she has had to struggle, scrap, and scratch for everything she has. Therefore, respect would be crucial to her, and she might feel the need to demand it instead of earning it. In the second situation, the manager solidified her self-worth by belittling other people. Unfortunately, the concept of rising above by pushing others down is all too common. Being overly social with the team increased her chances that one of them would write a comment on annual reviews, praising one manager over the other. This would allow her to convince herself that she must be better than her partner, thereby affirming her sense of self-worth.

Unfortunately, few people are genuinely grounded in their own self-esteem from childhood. Many have to build it for themselves and must therefore remain constantly vigilant to protect and maintain their self-esteem.

A plethora of excellent resources exist in books and on the internet to assist you in building and maintaining your own self-esteem, but you must put in the work. No one can do it for you. It is a uniquely individual effort for each of us. Let me share with you a few things that have been very helpful to me on this front:

Never compare yourself with anyone else. It is human nature to do so, but when we do, we constantly compare our weaknesses to their strengths. You will lose that comparison every time, so why would you do it? We all have our gifts. Each combination of human gifts is unique to that person. I am a gifted speaker, empathetic consultant, dynamite performer, and a heck of a decorator. I am also what I call "a hacker" vocalist. I'm okay in my car and at church, and I can slay at a karaoke bar. For years, when I was younger, I desperately wanted to be a leading actress on Broadway. If I'm honest with myself, I didn't have the voice for it. I actually didn't have the voice for leading roles in regional theater, and I spent way too many years comparing myself to those actresses who consistently beat me out of those leading roles. (I am a heck of a character actress, but that is beside the point.) Never compare yourself with anyone else. So long as I continued to compare myself to the ingénues & lyric sopranos, my self-esteem took hit after hit. Not until I stepped away from theater completely did my true gifts have room to shine, and my self-esteem grew and began working for me. (I may go back at some point and do some community theater just for giggles. There are many more character roles for women whose age is more interesting. If I do, however, it will be just for fun and not because I feel a need to prove anything to anyone – especially myself.)

In today's image-conscious society, we are constantly bombarded with the media's model of perfection, what we should look like, weigh, wear, and do. Images of the perceived perfect female form assault women from all directions. The implication is that variation from that stated perfection is somehow less valued. Men are bombarded with messages of athletic prowess, muscular build, and virility. Most of those images are not real. They have been photo-shopped, adjusted, tweaked, and enhanced. Comparing oneself to those images is a prescription for self-defeat every time.

As I travel, speak, and train, I encounter other excellent speakers. I never compare myself to them. They each have their gifts, and I have mine. I choose to compare myself only with my own best efforts, and then I strive to exceed those efforts. Never compare yourself with anyone else – only with your own best actions and intentions.

Keep a victory journal. Consider picking up an inexpensive spiral notebook (it doesn't have to be fancy and leather bound), and at the end of every day, write down something from that day that you did well. There's no scrimping allowed. There's never a day wherein you did *nothing* well. Once you get into that habit, add something special about yourself (not what you did, but who you *are*) every day. Again, no scrimping allowed. There can be no repeats of the previous day's entry. This forces you to see those things in yourself that deserve celebration. If you do this consistently and then look back over it after six to eight months, you will be amazed at how self-affirming it is.

Focus and build on your strengths. Each of us has gifts – things that we do well naturally. It's all too easy to dismiss such things emotionally because we don't have to work on them. We concentrate our attention on the "problem areas." We focus on the areas we are weak in and therefore need to improve upon. Don't get me wrong; I think continual growth is crucial. I just believe we spend too much time focusing on that, which can become very negative. As I said, I have a gift for speaking, performing, and decorating. I am *not* a numbers person. I will never be able to do long division in my head, and that's okay (that's what my husband is for). I can surround myself with people who are gifted in the areas that I'm not and utilize their strengths. It's a much better use of your emotional energy to acknowledge and build upon your strengths than to beat yourself up for things you are not as gifted at.

Speak only positive things to yourself. One of the most important aspects of maintaining rock-solid, positive self-esteem is what you say when you talk to yourself. (You'll notice I don't ask *if* you talk to yourself. We all do it. Some of us have a committee in the back of our heads!) It is a sad reality that people often will say to themselves what they would not dream of saying to other people. I have to admit the first time someone told me that I needed to speak positive thoughts to myself or write a personal affirmation, I said, "No thanks. I don't think so." It all sounded way too "Stuart Smalley" to me. (Stuart Smalley was a character from Saturday Night Live in the 1980s portrayed by Al Franken. Stuart was a member of several twelve-step programs, and regularly throughout the day, he would look at himself in the mirror and say, "Because I'm good enough. I'm nice enough, and gosh darn it, people like me.") The concept of becoming like that made me want to throw up. But affirmations *do* work, and they don't have to be nauseating. Sometimes we have to start where we are and write affirmations in small steps *toward* the self-esteem and confidence that we wish to be true. Begin by finding a positive statement you can believe and feel good about.

Then grow from there. The reality is that what you speak about, you bring about, and when we speak negative thoughts to ourselves, our subconscious believes it and sets about making it so. Start the self-esteem growth process here, with what you say when you talk to yourself. Speak only positive, nurturing thoughts to yourself.

Understanding one's own value, and the fact that this value is not affected by anything external, frees significant leaders to be humble. That may seem contradictory, but it's true, and the concept is crucial for significance. Furthermore, self-esteem and its resulting humility is a critical foundation for Essential #2, because we cannot treat others with respect if we don't respect ourselves.

Guidepost

A leader can be confident
and humble at the same time.
Arrogance grows out of a lack of self-esteem,
not an overabundance of it.

ESSENTIAL #2

Treat All People with Respect

There is a profound difference between respect for a person and treating a person with respect. My father, The Colonel, used to say, "You don't have to respect everyone, kiddo. You have no right to disrespect anyone, young lady."

In his book *How to Deal with Difficult People,* Paul Friedman made this intentional commitment: "I choose to treat this person with respect, whether or not I like what they think, say or do." I don't know if he intended that statement to be profound, but it was profound to me. I chose to take that intentional commitment on as one of my own. In any given situation, I would always want to be treated with respect and, therefore, can do nothing short of treating others the same. Even if someone is not treating me with respect, I choose to treat them with respect.

While every person will have their own concept of what treating others with respect looks like, I have a few baseline behaviors that help me stay on track. They include:

- Basic civility (please and thank you)
- Recognizing the inherent value in everyone I encounter
- Being present in the moment with others and not being distracted
- Listening without interrupting
- Taking responsibility for my mistakes
- Addressing others' mistakes with kindness
- Acknowledging others' efforts and achievements
- Making decisions based on what's right and appropriate, not on who I like
- Calling out disrespectful behavior when I see it
- Honoring physical boundaries
- Acknowledging others' right to a differing opinion
- Showing gratitude

Please don't misunderstand my intent here. I am not asking you to respect all people. There is a strong probability you will encounter someone who, for whatever reason – maybe their behavior, the choices they make, the words they choose, the way they treat others, differing ethics, etc. – you can in no way respect. Yet, significant leaders still choose to treat them with respect. The operative in the previous sentence is, of course, choose. It is an intentional choice that significant leaders make every day.

I believe there is no such thing as difficult people, only difficult behaviors. Some people will choose to exhibit difficult behaviors, but succumbing to such a label as "difficult people" is counterproductive because it cripples your ability to treat them with respect. This essential allows you to separate the person from the behavior or the issue at hand and enables you to address the problem without attacking the person. You have to be able to separate the behavior from the person so you can treat the person with respect.

This paradigm allows you a measure of security in knowing that your intentions are (usually) well-meaning. Few, if any, people feel no guilt whatsoever when they have mistreated someone else. Guilt robs you of your self-esteem. Therefore, when you disrespect someone, you open yourself up to guilt, even at a subconscious level, which will ultimately cripple your self-esteem. So even when others may be slogging through the gutters of pettiness or disrespect, significant leaders work hard to stay consistently on higher ground.

I used the phrase "usually well-meaning" because we all have moments when we stumble. Sometimes there are days when we just blow it entirely and fall right off that higher ground. Those are "oh poop" days. Then we have to wash our feet off, climb back up, and try again the next day. On other days, we have one foot up on higher ground and we hope no one notices we're dragging the other foot down in the muck. We do this because it feels good to have one foot in the gutter every now and then. Sometimes, if we're being honest, it feels good to gossip about other people, to say spiteful things just for the reaction, to bend or break the rules to see how much you can get away with, to expand a story to solidify your own position, to wallow in bitterness or refuse to forgive. Yet, at the end of the day, we still have to look ourselves in the eye and wash that foot off before sliding it into our nice clean sheets.

I shared this concept once with a group of mid-level managers I was training in the Midwest of the United States, and a younger gal from the back of the room piped up with, "Why? Why is it always us that has to be the bigger person? I'm freakin' tired of being the bigger person." That garnered some empathetic chuckles from around the room.

"Because we can," was my response. Significant leadership and walking the higher ground are not always easy. Sometimes it's no fun at all. It's a choice that has to be made every day. It's a commitment we make every morning when we look at ourselves in the mirror. Every day we commit to respect ourselves and others enough to climb up onto the higher ground and do the best we can that day.

I am the poster child for consistently slipping and trying to do better next time. I wish I could count the times I've stumbled and said or done something that demeaned or undermined someone else, whether intentionally or unintentionally. Each time, guilt came creeping in like a sticky black ooze to coat everything I've tried to accomplish afterward, and nothing subsequent was successful. I've watched in misery as the ooze attacked my self-esteem, which then began to crumble and dissolve. It has only been in admitting the mistake (again, intentional or unintentional), taking responsibility, and apologizing that the black ooze has receded and allowed me to rebuild my foundation.

Even now, as "enlightened" as I think myself to be, I sometimes hit a metaphorical pothole and trip, slipping off higher ground. Recently, I had arranged to meet my team for lunch at a local eatery to celebrate the successful completion of a large contract. My business manager and I arrived before the others and, because it was a lovely day, we decided to wait for the rest outside the restaurant. A black pickup pulled up and parked in the handicapped spot right in front of the restaurant. I looked, almost casually, for the handicapped plate or a mirror tag – neither of which existed. A man with no apparent disability climbed out of the pickup truck and headed toward the door.

My business manager made eye contact with the man and said, "Are you handicapped?"

The man scoffed, tapped his head to indicate his brain, and said, "Up here."

"Apparently," was my manager's under-his-breath response.

Unfortunately, at that point, I started a slow burn. One of my most challenging emotional stumbling blocks and quickest flash points is people who believe they are somehow more important than others or more important than the rules. Accessible parking spots are reserved for people with disabilities for a reason, and I find few things as inconsiderate and disrespectful as non-disabled people using those spots. I wish there were an immediate response number, like a parking control 9-1-1, for such an occasion so that the police could immediately issue a prompt and grossly expensive ticket. (But I digress.)

The others arrived, and we walked into the restaurant just in time to encounter the man walking out with his to-go order. I shot him a glare. He flashed a cocky, sideways grin at me and said, "Thanks for watching my truck for me."

Slow burn met flash point, and I called the man a name I choose not to repeat here. I don't use profanity; indeed, I preach against using profanity. Therefore, hearing it out of my mouth caught my team totally off guard. It also was not said softly, so I attracted the attention of all the other nearby patrons in the restaurant. At that moment, I fell utterly off higher ground. I stooped down to his level and gave him control of my significance. I had shifted the focus of the moment from celebrating my team to shining a spotlight on a stranger's bad behavior. He was wrong. I was more wrong, though, because regardless of how he might have treated me or what he might have done, I had betrayed standards that I had set for myself. It was disrespectful to him and equally, if not more, disrespectful to the team I had come to celebrate.

Furthermore, I expect that my doing so did not get my desired result. I can presume with some certainty that the man did not drive away from the restaurant that day thinking, "Ya know, my parking there really upset that woman. I was wrong and, therefore, will not park in a handicapped spot again."

A colleague subsequently asked me what the higher-ground, significant action would have been in that situation. I could have said nothing at all, realizing that there would always be people trying to skirt the rules and knowing they would eventually get censured in some manner. I could have called the police immediately and hoped they would arrive before he left. I could have written down his license plate number to give to the officer if they did not come in time to issue the man a ticket. I could have approached the man calmly, assertively, and in a controlled manner and explained why a non-disabled person parking in a handicapped spot is so disrespectful. Any of those options would have been a better choice. The only result was me having to metaphorically wash my feet off (and my mouth out!), apologize to my team for my offensive language, and climb back up on the higher ground to try again. The climb that particular day felt like Mt. Everest for me.

Treating all people with respect, even in the most difficult of circumstances, does not make someone weak. Quite the opposite – choosing to treat someone with respect in the face of disrespect shows extreme strength of character. You can't lead someone if they feel disrespected by you or if they see you treating others disrespectfully.

Guidepost

Significant leaders make the daily choice to treat all people with respect at all times, regardless of what they think, say, or do.

ESSENTIAL #3

Act with Integrity at All Times

Simply put, integrity is doing what is right because it's right, every time, whether anyone is looking or not. Significant leaders are intentional in that integrity. This includes choices they make in their professional and personal lives and how they treat people who can ostensibly do nothing for them. It also includes financial decisions and consistency in their commitments, among many other things.

The Colonel often said, "It takes a lifetime to build a reputation of trust, kiddo, and only one 'ah poop' to bring it down." (Poop was not the word he used, but we'll run with it.) We've all seen people with enormous capability, strong results, and even sometimes good intent who unfortunately go about what they're doing in a dishonest or corrupt way. It's a "the end justifies the means" mentality. Unfortunately, the end does not engender trust if the means are unethical. Personal and professional integrity is crucial for building team trust. To most people, integrity means honesty – telling the truth and leaving the right impression. Additional qualities involved in integrity could include congruence, humility, and courage.

In his book *The Speed of Trust*, Stephen M. R. Covey identified two aspects of trust (which can be likened to integrity): cognitive and affective. Cognitive trust is based on confidence in another person's accomplishments, skills, and reliability. This is trust from the head. On the other hand, affective trust arises from feelings of security, emotional closeness, empathy, or friendship. This trust is from the heart.

The behaviors Covey associated with cognitive trust (integrity) are reliability, accountability, development, and continuous learning. The behaviors Covey associated with affective trust (integrity) are empathy, self-awareness, inclusion, and openness. When a person can consistently earn both cognitive and affective trust – that is, trust from the head and the heart – they have the opportunity to make a real difference in the lives of others and be genuinely significant.

In my experience, a couple of behaviors speak most strongly to one's character and integrity.

The first is truthfulness. Folks, always tell the truth – even when the truth is difficult.

I've discovered the hard way in my life that telling the truth is easier and creates less stress. I say "the hard way" because (full disclosure) I was a practiced liar for many years. I am a recovering bulimic. I have an eating disorder called bulimia nervosa and have been in sustained recovery for 38 years so far. Eating disorders are addictions that manifest themselves with food or the control of food as our focus. So, I use the word addict universally. All addicts, at some level, are practiced liars. It's a symptom and a natural part of addiction. We lie about what we've done, what we haven't done, who we were with, what we ate, and what we purged. Addicts lie. I could say that I came by it naturally (and to a certain extent, I did; addiction is hereditary). I watched my alcoholic mother lie about whether or not she'd been drinking, where she'd been, or what she'd been doing. It might be easy to blame my lying on genetics. To do so, however, would discount my responsibility. Every person makes a choice, sometimes daily, as to whether they are going to be a truthful person or a deceitful person. When I was in treatment for my bulimia, I finally made a choice to commit to the truth no matter what. I visualized it this way: I placed an imaginary door in front of me. On one side was the addict who lied. On the other side was recovery – wherein I always tell the truth. Mentally, I walked through that door, closed it, deadbolted it, and then bricked over it for good measure. Once on this side of the door, I had a profound discovery: the truth is easier. When you tell a lie (big or small), you always carry the burden of remembering what you said to whom. Lies grow and propagate other lies, which requires still more space in your brain. Eventually and assuredly, the memory cells fill to capacity and begin to leak. I just don't have enough room in my brain anymore to carry even one fabricated story, much less multiple ones! The truth never changes; therefore, it doesn't require as much memory space. Furthermore, the truth doesn't have to adapt to serve the purpose of the liar. The truth just is.

Any parent will tell you that children usually lie to avoid disappointing their parents but fail to realize that it is the lie itself a parent finds more disappointing than whatever behavior the child might be lying about. So it is also with a leader and their team. If a team finds its leader caught in a falsehood, the fabric of trust will be torn permanently. Conversely, when you develop the reputation of someone who always tells the truth, then you can comfortably expect the truth from others in your conversations.

Furthermore, I have found it beneficial to stop and think before I open my mouth, so that I am confident about what the actual truth is. While you think, don't elaborate. It is a natural tendency of human nature that as we think, we tend to add our own perceptions into the mix, and the perceived truth tends to expand. Don't do this. Trim the truth down to the barest minimum of known facts.

The bottom line is that people need to believe they can trust you to tell them the truth. So, even when the truth is hard, always tell the truth.

A second behavior that speaks to one's character is consistency. The Colonel said, "If you can't be consistent, kid, you can't be trusted." Consistency is a critical factor in leadership, and inconsistency is a pothole that will quickly undermine your credibility.

When The Colonel was initially stationed at the Flight Dynamics Laboratory at Wright Patterson AFB, he was in the queue for a promotion that he believed would take him through to his first star. Dinner table conversation (overheard by children who were seen but not heard) centered around the perception that the person with the decision power didn't like Dad.

"That shouldn't matter," he avowed. "He doesn't have to like me. I don't particularly like him either. He has to recognize that I am the best person for the job and do what's right for the division and the future of the Air Force. We should be able to work together and be productive regardless of whether we like each other."

Apparently Dad was right, and it didn't ultimately matter, because he got the promotion to Division Chief.

A few months later, he was assessing potential candidates for Assistant Division Chief to fill the post he had recently vacated. I again overheard dinner table conversation as Dad whined, "Geez, he's smart and capable, and his record is great . . . it's just that, God, I hate his mannerisms. His whole personality rubs me the wrong way. I just don't know if I can work with him."

The whole "seen but not heard" thing was never my strong point, so I (at all of 13 years old) piped up at that point: "Ya know, Daddy, it's possible he doesn't like you either, but he still posted for the job. I thought that you didn't have to like someone to be able to work with them." Silence. For a long moment, I was unsure if I would be sent to my room and grounded for the comment.

"You are absolutely right, Lauren Ann. If I can't be consistent in what I believe, say, and do, I can't be trusted to run the division. Thank you for reminding me of that."

As leaders, what we say will always be recorded, if not on audio or camera, certainly in the minds of those we are commissioned to represent. That is why it's crucial to consider the potential ramifications of what we say and do before speaking or acting. If what we say we believe, what we say is right, and what we say is best for our staff changes on a whim to suit our purposes or our agenda, it was never trustworthy in the first place. If you can't be consistent, you can't be trusted.

The third behavior that speaks to a person's character is how they treat everyone, especially those who seemingly can do nothing for them. Indeed, the measure of a person's integrity is almost completely based on this. You see, it's easy to treat people with respect if we want or need something from them, or if they are perceived to be in a higher position. But it's how we treat the rest of the population –

those who report to us or who are lower in the organizational chart, those who seemingly can do nothing for us – that really defines us.

When I first joined the National Speakers Association as a brand-new, emerging speaker, I was naive and eager to learn the ins and outs of the speaking business. NSA was founded on the premise that, as we help each other get better, the speaking industry as a whole gets better and grows as a result. During my first six months in the association, I met many people who had achieved what I was hoping to achieve. Some dismissed me entirely as not worth their time, while others saw me as a rookie target and were eager to sell me their consulting services on how I could become a million-dollar speaker. Some, however, took a genuine interest in me with an authentic desire to help me build my potential. They offered their time, expertise, insights, contacts, and marketing resources to help me build to a level where I would (theoretically) not need them anymore. Those shining examples have never expected anything but friendship in return. Of course, they have become some of my dearest friends, and I will always need them in that capacity. I respect and admire them a great deal.

Now that I am more well-established and have achieved a portion of the success I aspire to, I am often approached by emerging speakers wanting to "pick my brain" and ask questions. I always take the time to offer whatever wisdom I can. I gauge how I treat the up-and-comers based on how I was treated and endeavor to make them feel valued while giving freely to help them build their success.

Furthermore, many of those who dismissed me initially now want to get to know me and build collaborations or partnerships. Although they may not remember me from "back then," if I were to collaborate with them, I have a pretty good idea of how they will treat smaller-fish clients or prospects who, perhaps, have no further connections or marketing value for them. So, I pick and choose who I respond to very carefully.

How you treat those who report to you and those who seemingly can do nothing for you is a measure of your character. Treat all people with the same standard of respect because people notice, and they remember.

It was once said (by the great philosopher Anonymous) that "integrity is what happens in the dark." There are thousands upon thousands of individual ethical choices that significant leaders need to make (seemingly in the dark) every day. Still, they are always guided by the principle of doing what is right because it's right, every time, whether anyone is looking or not.

A team may not fully understand their leader's vision; they may disagree with their leader's decisions. A team member doesn't even have to like their leader very much. But, a team must trust the character of their leader, or they will refuse to be led.

Guidepost

Before your people trust you, they have to know that you are competent and have integrity.
They will forgive a failure in competence.
A failure in integrity will kill that trust every time.

ESSENTIAL #4

Open Your Mind to New Possibilities

There was no question in our household that both of Dad's daughters would go to college and get their degrees. (Dad had three advanced degrees! Who can compete with that?) But it wasn't just about getting a college education. To Dad, it was about learning from every situation. You have to be willing to learn and grow if you want to lead. You have to be open to new ideas, information, and possibilities. Leadership is not a stagnant profession. It requires continuous learning, from colleagues, mentors, those in different departments, and from your team.

Only an open mind is a growing mind. A closed mind cannot grow, and a closed mind cannot lead. Significant leaders recognize they don't know everything or have all the answers. Only a bloated ego and a closed mind believe they have unlimited knowledge, awareness, or understanding. Be purposeful in tapping into the expertise and strengths of others, even if that means learning what *not* to do from others. This doesn't have to apply just to your industry either. Learn about something that, at first glance, may have nothing to do with your field, or learn about things that bring you joy. This allows you to see, embrace and seize upon opportunities for your team that you would not have been able to visualize alone.

Sometimes, opening our minds to new possibilities means we have to be willing to learn from our mistakes or misfortunes, make adjustments, and keep moving on. The Colonel used to say, "Use what you've got, kid, and just show up. Stumbling block or stepping stone, it's your choice. What's it gonna be?" Many things have happened so far in the 21st century that could easily be considered major stumbling blocks (and I don't mean to minimize any of them), but what if we looked at them from a different direction? How will you turn even one of your stumbling blocks into a stepping stone?

When I was a young girl of six or seven, Dad spent countless hours and what my mother called an "obscene amount of money" constructing a remote-control model airplane. Back then, they were called "radio-controlled," and the technology was brand new – cutting edge for its day. I remember helping to paint the wings with a black and white feather pattern and sitting with him in the garage as he worked on it every evening. This thing was massive. It had a six-foot wingspan and took up all of the space in the garage during the year and a half that Dad spent building it.

I remember the excitement and anticipation on that fall morning when we all piled into the Jeep, pulling the plane on a flatbed trailer behind us, and headed out to the mesa south of Chandler, AZ. This was the day we would test "the bird" on her maiden flight.

It took a good couple of hours to get everything ready. Mom and the kids were on runway duty. It was our job, using rakes and brooms, to clear rocks and debris from a stretch of relatively flat desert so nothing would get in the way of a smooth takeoff. Dad had to check the wind patterns and then recheck them. He made sure the receivers were working and then checked the wind (again). He set the cameras (both still and 8mm) to record the event for posterity before giving one final check on the wind. Finally, everything was ready.

Dad picked up the control box and fired up the propeller, saying, "Here goes nothing." He slowly pushed the throttle lever forward, and the plane started rolling down the makeshift runway. It seemed that before we could blink, the bird was in the air and flying!

And flying . . . And flying . . . And flying . . .

Mom squinted into the sun, "Are you gonna turn it around before it's out of range?" We watched it get smaller and smaller in the distance.

"Um, I'm not quite sure I know how to do that. I didn't think that far. I didn't think she would actually fly today."

So there we all stood, watching a year and a half of Dad's life (and an obscene amount of money) fly off into the sunset, never to be seen again. Oh, we drove for hours across the desert looking for it until well after dark, but we never actually found the bird.

Although Mom never let Dad forget that first lost "toy," the lessons we learned from that costly mistake were invaluable. We learned that the things we don't anticipate are the very things that will go wrong. We learned always to have a backup plan. We learned to expect the unexpected. (And Dad learned to never again tell Mom how much he had spent on his many projects!)

Most importantly, Dad's initial R.C. plane debacle allowed him to open his mind to new possibilities. For him, it was not a stumbling block but a stepping stone. It inspired him to build a second one, and many more after that. He kept at it, always looking for new ways to improve the design. With each new model, he would adapt the wing structure or sculpt his own airfoils for the wings. He tried hundreds of different materials and combinations. Some worked well, some didn't, but each iteration taught him valuable lessons. And when he became Division Chief for the Air Force Flight Dynamics Laboratory, that tenacity paid off, as he and his team designed new materials, technologies, and structures for drones and planes that are still in the air today, like the B2-Stealth Bomber and the F-Series Fighter Jets.

Significant leaders understand that what has worked in the past can act as a starting point; however, by the mere fact that it was in the past, they know it may not be the best choice going forward.

Looking at new ways of doing things, taking different routes to the desired endpoint, and allowing alternative voices to lead the conversation or thought process are all necessary elements in bringing about the best result. Communicating to your team that you know you cannot have all the answers empowers each individual member to contribute their knowledge and expertise toward the solution or the desired outcome.

What stumbling blocks have you faced or maybe are facing right now? (And I know, some may be bigger than seeing a few thousand dollars and a year and a half of your time fly off into the distance, never to be seen again.) How can you look at them differently? What minor adjustments can you implement that will make a difference and turn them into stepping stones? How will you take what you've learned and use that to benefit others first, to be of service? Significant leaders consistently ask themselves, "How can I use this situation to open my mind to new possibilities? How can I take lessons from the past to look at the current situation differently? How can I tap into the strengths of others to shift my perspective? How can I use what I am learning to help others grow or make their path easier?"

Once we stop learning, we start dying. The reality is this, folks: half of what you think you know now will be obsolete and, therefore, worthless ten years from now. So, open your mind to new possibilities and never stop learning.

Guidepost

"Ya gotta keep asking questions.
Otherwise, you end up stagnant.
Nothing will kill ya quicker than being stagnant."
– THE COLONEL

ESSENTIAL #5

Craft a Vision

While crafting a vision may seem like Leadership 101 material, its importance is more profound than it might seem at a surface level. While it is undoubtedly crucial for the leader to establish and communicate the team's objective goal and their priorities in getting to that goal, significant leaders go beyond the superficial layer. Ideally, a leader would gather input from the team and craft a vision that incorporates their input into the story of the ultimate vision. You see, a team can be committed to the organization, getting along well, and doing great work, but if they aren't moving toward a shared vision, they are not as effective as they could be.

A friend of mine, a former pastor, once said in jest, "If you want to get a congregation moving and serving, go into debt and take on a big capital project – especially one that seems nearly unattainable." Amazing things happen when there is a shared vision and everyone understands it can't be accomplished without each person's effort. You see, when people come together to address a massive challenge or achieve a big goal, one bigger than anyone could accomplish alone, leaders emerge, new talents are discovered, and everyone finds their role.

The Colonel's time in the Air Force was entirely a collaboration in support of a more significant cause. Early in his career, Dad worked in ordinance effectiveness and facility survivability. Those were really big words for a six-year-old daughter to get her mouth, much less her brain, around! But as Dad explained it, he designed bombs that would have the maximum effect on a target with minimal collateral damage (that is, impact on the surrounding area). He also designed buildings and shelters to withstand the enemy's bombing raids. Later, as Division Chief of the Flight Dynamics Laboratory, his staff developed the lightweight advanced composite, radar-absorbing materials with which the stealth bombers and F-series fighters are constructed. His career was wholly focused on leading teams toward a singular vision: making those deployed in harm's way more accurate, effective, and safe, so they could come home to their families. That was a pretty big cause, and he made sure each member of his staff knew how important their work was, where they fit into the vision, and why it mattered to each of them individually.

Like players on a football team (I *love* American football), every member of your team has a specific job to do. On a football team, some may be rushing, some may be blocking, some may be tackling, etc., but they all have a shared vision, a common objective – and that is to get the ball into the end zone and score (or prevent the other team from doing so). Without that common objective to work toward, the individual players' skills would result in nothing more than just a bunch of people being physically aggressive with each other on a grassy field.

So, one of the primary jobs of leadership is providing that shared vision for where the team is going and what it will look like when they get there. Each member of your team needs to know both the individual parts they play (the "what are you working on?") and how they will share the benefit at the end (the "what are we all working toward?"). Tell them how it will feel when we achieve "X" together.

A compelling vision should have a few key elements. First, it needs to be future-focused. A vision lives in the future, not the past. It's about progress toward a goal, improvement, growth, or specific success. This usually requires a shift in paradigm for most new leaders. Coming up through the ranks as an individual contributor or project manager, we're focused on and rewarded for execution and results. These are things that exist primarily in the present. Managers are considered most successful if they can tackle the critical objectives of the day and resolve issues in the moment. When crafting a vision, however, one must primarily be looking forward to a future that lies further ahead. The leader has to be able to see it themselves first in order to orient everyone else toward it.

Second, the vision must be positive. No one wants to run toward a bleak future. Therefore, significant leaders communicate possibilities. Rather than fixating on problems, they visualize solutions. This *doesn't* mean a vision shouldn't be based on reality. If the current reality is bleak, the picture may not be sunshine and pots of gold at the end of a rainbow, but it needs to be less gloomy than the current reality. Acknowledge the existing challenges, but rather than wallowing in them, get focused instead. This concentrated positivity is contagious and can inspire others to be equally positive and committed. When times get tough, a targeted vision allows a team to pull together and push through. It is not a leader's job to be constantly upbeat and joyous, because challenges and setbacks are part of the job. The vision, though, needs to be positive and point in an inspiring direction.

Compelling visions are also intentionally inclusive. They paint a picture wherein everyone has a meaningful role. Sometimes our team can't always see how their work matters to the greater whole. The "cog in the wheel" syndrome undermines innovation, creativity, and job satisfaction. An inclusive vision helps every employee see how their work matters and is fundamental to the larger objectives. It tells them where their piece of the puzzle fits. This may seem obvious to you, as you have been living and crafting the vision for some time. That doesn't mean others can see it easily. For the dream to come to life, each individual must see themselves included.

In addition, for a vision to grow off of a piece of paper and into the hearts and minds of your team, you have to keep the dream alive through consistent action. A vision that's future-focused, positive, and inclusive but rarely discussed is pointless. Many visions fail because leaders get bored of talking about them. Therefore, a vision needs to be active and kinetic. Discuss it in meetings, casual conversations, and presentations at every opportunity. When an individual or team's work or achievement aligns with the vision, recognize that achievement publicly. The vision should be woven into the fabric of daily work.

Part of keeping a vision active is recognizing that it is constantly evolving – because we all learn and adapt as we go. Your team is not looking for certainty or set-in-stone absolutes. They're looking for a path forward, something to believe in and work toward.

Finally, and most importantly, your vision needs to be personal to each employee. Dig deep into both the vision and what you know about your individual team members to create a moment in time for them. What will it look like for each unique team member when the objective is achieved? Why should it matter to them individually? How will it benefit them or someone/something that matters to them? Focus on the why behind the what for each person.

It's important to acknowledge that unless you're the CEO, the vision doesn't just come from you but is connected to the organization's larger mission and purpose. You may be constrained by objectives and priorities already decided by someone higher on the organizational chart. Even so, significant leaders take the roadmap for the company and make it relevant for their team. And because we don't just exist within our companies, a good leader also provides context for the outside environment. In this way, a vision creates shared meaning for others. Significant leaders know that they see more and have access to more information because of their position, and they remember that others don't have the advantage of the same perspective. Do not assume people already know this context! It's better to be redundant than to keep people guessing.

When you focus on a progressive, positive, inclusive, active, and personalized vision, the team will grab that vision and start running toward it. In fact, it's not always necessary for the leader to know the exact processes used to achieve that vision, especially if the team you've gathered is empowered to make their own decisions and find their own path to the outcome you have established. Furthermore, if you can communicate why your team wants (or needs) to do something – the "what's in it for them" – they will often create the means for achieving that task, project, or vision on their own. It's imperative, therefore, that you get to know your team well, because one person's "why" may be very different from another person's. One size does not necessarily fit all; each individual's puzzle piece is separate and fits uniquely into the whole picture. They will work hard to bring that vision to life when they understand why.

> ### *Guidepost*
>
> Significant leaders focus on the **why** behind the what when casting a vision for their team.

ESSENTIAL #6

Communicate Respectfully

The greatest hindrance to growth in any career and in any organization is poor communication up and down the ladder. Whether it be conflict within an organization, poor production, or even major crises – if you dissect them down to their initial root causes, you will find they could have been avoided if there had just been effective communication from the start.

Most people believe that a leader's first communication priority is to be assertive and clear. In an emergency, when there is imminent danger, this is absolutely the only objective, but in any other situation, it is not.

Embracing respectful communication is easier when we understand our objective as communicators (and as leaders). As I see it, our objective is three-fold: all people must (first) feel safe and treated with respect in our presence while we (second) stand our own ground and (third) get our message across. Let's dig into each of these three components a little bit deeper.

When I say "all people feel safe," I mean physically safe, certainly, but also intellectually and emotionally safe. So much of the harassment that happens in our workplaces is rooted in intangibles. There is no physical threat, but emotional or intellectual suffering is oppressive. This could include sexual harassment. It could also include (but is not limited to) bullying, offensive jokes, slurs, epithets or name-calling, intimidation, ridicule or mockery, insults or put-downs, offensive objects or pictures, and interference with work performance. All of these could create an environment wherein someone would not feel intellectually or emotionally safe.

If you have ever been in a situation where you did not feel safe (physically, intellectually, or emotionally), I would venture to say you were not enthusiastic about furthering communication! By the same token, if you ever felt disrespected in a conversation, you would not feel like continuing it. This is why we must start here with our objective.

The second arm of our objective is standing our own ground. Having the courage of conviction and the ability not to be steamrolled by someone with a stronger or louder voice is crucial. This does not mean we need to be bull-headed or not listen to opposing opinions; it simply means we are able to hold on to our point or our message (if we believe very strongly in it) when under pressure to change it.

The third arm of our objective is getting our message across. This means we are clear, free of ambiguity, and concise, and we utilize language appropriate to the situation and easily understood by the listener.

This approach to our objective as communicators is admittedly backward from how most people approach the subject. Most communication experts (even many of my well-respected and beloved colleagues) will tell you that the most crucial component of communication is to be clear and understood. I have met many people who are very clear in their communication – and also leave a trail of human ruin behind them as they do business, which is unproductive and unsustainable for long-term effectiveness. That is why I feel compelled to approach it from the other direction. Our goal should always be to allow all people to feel safe and treated with respect in our presence first, while we stand our own ground and get our message across. I am unwilling to compromise on any of these three, and they have to come in that order.

Once our objective is clear, every other skill we utilize to communicate is filtered through it. Some of those skills include:

Emotional control – Simply put, if you are not in control of your emotions and are not objective, you lose effectiveness as a communicator and a leader. Although some people tend to be more emotional than others, emotions in themselves are not a bad thing. Emotions play a vital role in our lives by allowing us to express complex combinations of psychological states, which enables us to resolve them. There are no good emotions, and there are no bad emotions. Emotions just are. Nonetheless, having a handle on them is vital so that we control them – they are not controlling us. Significant leaders understand the difference between reacting and responding and endeavor to *respond* whenever possible.

Nonverbal communication – You are always saying something, whether you are speaking or not. Your nonverbal communication includes everything that communicates for you without words – your posture, approachability, eye contact, gestures, and personal proximity. All non-verbal factors can be controlled and utilized to ensure that our unspoken signals are in harmony and do not conflict with the message we want to send. Furthermore, our nonverbal communication often has the most substantial effect on allowing all people to feel safe and treated with respect in our presence.

Listening – This is the most underutilized, under-appreciated, and under-practiced communication skill. My experience has shown that listening is the primary shortfall in most leaders' communication proficiency. This is unfortunate because, in business as in life, we automatically feel a bias toward those whom we believe are listening to us, and we are prejudiced against those we think are not. We want that bias in our favor so we can be most effective. Besides, every human being I have met (thus far in my life) was designed with two ears and only one mouth. The problem is we don't use them in the correct proportion!

Respectful wording – For many years, I taught the spectrum of three basic ways to communicate: passive, aggressive, and assertive. If you are passive, people tend to steamroll right over you. You often feel unheard and discounted, leading to emotional internalizing and burnout. If you are aggressive, you tend to repel more people than you attract, which is unproductive and can lead to resentment among coworkers. I taught that "truly successful people are assertive." About ten years ago, though,

I began challenging myself to a higher standard: respectful communication. Therefore, I have no choice but to challenge my audiences and clients to the same new standard. My experience has shown me that while respectful communication is always assertive, not all assertive communication is necessarily respectful. The best definition of respectful communication I have ever seen came from a book called *Power Phrases* by Meryl Runion. (I wish I could take credit for it, but I simply can't articulate it better than she did.) Runion defined effective communication this way: "Say what you mean. Mean what you say, and don't be mean when you say it." That is profound in its simplicity and a model everyone can remember.

Flexing – Flexing how we communicate is a skill that can transform an excellent communicator into a great communicator and a successful manager into a significant leader. If our goal as communicators is to allow all people to feel safe and treated with respect in our presence while we stand our own ground and get our message across, then our job as communicators is to meet people in their own comfort zone, not assume they are going to jump into ours.

Wouldn't it make everything easier if we could offer all information in a manner that is easy for the recipient to understand, absorb and act upon? The reality is this: if I know more about myself and my communication comfort zone than you know about yourself and your communication comfort zone, I control the communication (and often the outcome). Flexing ourselves to diverse communication involves all manner of diversity, which might also include, but is not limited to, culture, values, religion, sexual orientation, personalities, gender, generations, and many other factors too numerous to list.

Communicating respectfully is not about just speaking what we think. We need to do so in such a manner that others hear what we mean. It's no accident that I ended up as a professional speaker. I spent most of my youth hearing people tell me to stop talking! It wasn't until much later in my life that I realized there is a fundamental difference between talking and communicating. Truly communicating respectfully compels others to internalize or act upon what you have said.

Significant leaders consistently communicate so that the team feels seen, heard, supported, empathized with, and able to internalize and act upon the message. We should strive for an empathy bond such that, even when we word things poorly (as we all inevitably do now and then), our team can hear the message behind the words and understand what we truly mean. That's a tall order but one we should be continually working toward.

Communicating respectfully helps solidify the influence a leader has with their team. Influence is a golden intangible. It happens when all communication factors come together, through consistent practice and discipline, and work in harmony on the solid structure of mutual respect.

I have often had some of my more fast-paced, results-oriented clients say something to the effect of, "Look, I don't have time for all this sugar-coated, nicey-nicey stuff. It's not my job to hold their hands. It's my job to make sure they do their jobs. They should just do their jobs. That's what they get paid to do." Yes, that is what they get paid to do. Yet, my experience has proven to me that if you take the time to filter your communication through the lens of our goal as communicators (and leaders) and flex how you communicate to meet them at their comfort zone, your results will be better. That's what we are looking for, isn't it? Results? Furthermore, communicating through this filter allows your team, unit, circle of influence, and those who follow you to feel more comfortable, respected, fulfilled, and encouraged in their working environment.

Guidepost

"Say what you mean. Mean what you say, and don't be mean when you say it."

— MERYL RUNION

ESSENTIAL #7

Lead by Example

I sincerely believe there are three and only three ways to lead: by example, by example, and (you guessed it) by example. Ralph Waldo Emerson said, "What you do speaks so loudly I cannot hear what you say."

Significant leadership is not about pushing people toward excellence; it's about demonstrating excellence. Rather than saying to your team, "You can do this," leading by example communicates that "we can do this together." While the former is supportive and encouraging, the latter strengthens trust and builds connection.

It's a common but misguided perception that once you've made it to the top, things get easier because you can relax and let other people do the work. That is an excellent recipe for losing your spot at the top. Being a leader is hard work – all the time. It is also rewarding – most of the time. And that "most of the time" makes the rest of the time worth it.

The Colonel loved this quote, which he said was originally from General Douglas MacArthur: "Never send your troops in where you are not willing to go, and never ask them to do something you are unwilling to do yourself." While doing everything yourself is not a characteristic of leadership, if you have never been where you're sending your team (metaphorically), you have no basis to guide them on the journey.

I have a friend who is a fitness trainer. He spends eight to ten hours a day in the gym with his clients, guiding them to their fitness goals. Every evening after dinner, he goes back to the gym to work out himself. I asked him about that one time.

"You're in the gym all day long. Don't you get tired of being there?"

He said, "Of course I do. But my clients won't put work in that I haven't put in before them. Can you imagine if I was fifty pounds overweight, always out of breath, and looking like the most I could curl is a donut up to my mouth? Would you believe me when I told you that you could achieve your personal best? Would you push just a little bit harder when I encourage you to? I put the work in on myself, so I can guide and encourage you to put the work in on yourself."

Then he told me to do another set of ten.

Everyone watches those in leadership positions, looking for both behaviors to emulate and inconsistencies in their behavior to criticize. You have to be aware of and prepared for that.

At one point in my career, I was highly involved in a couple of Chambers of Commerce in my area, functioning as an ambassador for both. As my travel load increased, I knew I needed to trim down my obligations to be more effective for my business. The decision of which chamber to release, though, was difficult. Both had their unique merits, and I had friends and colleagues in both.

One of the chambers had just gone through a lengthy search process to find its new staff president. This new president talked about how valuable the membership was to her and how eager she was to get to know every one of us personally. I read everything she'd written, trying to glimpse her character and authenticity, knowing that she would invariably set the standard for that chamber going forward.

At her first event, I introduced myself to her. We had a brief conversation, during which she consistently looked over my shoulder at other people in the room. Though she met my eyes periodically on her way from looking over one shoulder to the other, it was never meaningful or focused.

At breakfast, she said a few words from the podium and then introduced the speaker, who was a member of the chamber. After mispronouncing his name, she gushed apologies and said she couldn't wait to hear what he had to say. The featured speaker was a banker, not a professional speaker, and it was apparent that he was very nervous. About two minutes into his presentation, the back of my brain was distracted by a conversation going on at the table behind me. Not a casual, "I missed that, what did he say?" kind of comment, but a fully engaged, oblivious conversation. As a professional speaker, I certainly could hold my own in that situation, but the distraction quite obviously flustered this fellow.

I turned to see who was being so rude and carrying on this conversation. (Okay, let's be honest; I turned to give them "the glare.") The oblivious conversation was coming from the new president. That was the instant the decision of which chamber to let go of was made. With her actions, she had communicated how she would treat the members of the chamber and the level of courtesy the membership could expect from her. The example she was leading by was contrary to her words and her commitment, and I chose to release my membership in that particular chamber in order to focus my available time on my other chamber membership.

When a leader talks about how the team should treat each other respectfully and then disrespects someone, all credibility is lost. The team gets the message very clearly that it's actually okay to disrespect each other, regardless of what was said. If the leader rallies the team together for a "we've all got to work harder" speech and then takes the afternoon off, the message is very different than what was intended. The team will seize upon that inconsistency, and trust is fractured – perhaps permanently.

If the company policy establishes strict guidelines on the use of company credit cards, but the leader regularly uses their card for personal expenses believing that "it's okay so long as I pay it back promptly," the team will see that as hypocrisy and be unwilling to follow company guidelines themselves.

On the other hand, when the team sees their leader treating each person with respect, they will be more likely to follow that example. When the leader says, "We've all got to work a bit harder to make this happen," and then rolls their shirtsleeves up, digs in, and works harder themselves, the team will be motivated to work harder as well. Leading by example actively demonstrates the value of your team's work by taking some of the load on your own shoulders. Because you have shown that you are fully invested in the team's initiatives, that example fosters higher levels of trust, engagement, and emotional buy-in.

This question should always be in a leader's mind: "If someone I value saw this behavior (or heard what I just said), would that make me feel proud, or would that make me feel like I should have done (or said) something differently?" Leaders do more than the rest of the team – usually behind the scenes – not for their own achievement or accolades but for the team's benefit. Leadership is often a lonely road that requires letting go of privilege to help others grow. Significant leaders are consistently intentional in exhibiting the behaviors they would expect from their team.

Guidepost

In leadership, there is no space for,
"Do as I say, not as I do."
Your team is always watching and
will follow your example,
whether you want them to or not.

ESSENTIAL #8

Celebrate the Results Of Others

Legendary college football coach Bear Bryant often said, "If we win big, the boys did a heck of a job. If we squeak by with a win, we've all got some work to do. If we lose, it's all on me."

According to a survey completed by Microsoft in January of 2022,[3] one of the primary reasons employees leave their jobs is that they don't feel appreciated, yet 65 percent of employees haven't received any form of recognition over the last year.

Near the end of my term as president of a non-profit foundation award committee, I jokingly told The Colonel how the awards should all go to me because I had worked harder than anyone else on the committee or in the arts community that particular year. "Wrong," was The Colonel's response. "As president, it's your job to work harder than anyone else. Don't look for recognition for that. It's part and parcel of the title."

It is normal and natural to give the leader credit and accolades for a team's accomplishments. Few people step into leadership because they want to hide in the shadows, and I don't think wanting to be acknowledged is about an over-inflated ego. It's a relatively normal and natural desire to be recognized for our hard work and successes. Leaders, though, need to rise above that very genuine desire. Accepting credit for the team's results communicates to the individual team members that their effort was not noticed or was insignificant.

Dad continued, "Instead of looking for credit, you should be entirely focused on who you should be giving credit to. You didn't achieve this year's success on your own. Far from it, kid. It's not the leader's job to get the recognition but to give it. Besides, if you are always focused on helping your team look good, they will invariably make you look good."

Leaders need to be constantly aware that recognition comes in many forms. It isn't just about implementing employee programs or distributing expensive gifts; it's about bringing out the best in people and, thereby, improving their commitment and performance.

In that same Microsoft survey, employees were asked what types of recognition they've found most memorable. The top five methods were:

- Public recognition or acknowledgment
- Private recognition from a boss, peer, or customer
- Receiving or obtaining high-level ratings, evaluations, or reviews
- Promotion or increase in scope and responsibility
- Monetary awards, pay increases, trips, etc.

As you can see, the top two most memorable and impactful forms of employee recognition have very little to do with money; their value comes from the format, quality, and distribution channel. You can use public recognition to celebrate an achievement that has a broader business impact. It brings visibility to and honors the efforts of an individual or team, and it can be used as a training moment to highlight the value of the team's work in the bigger picture organization-wide.

Not everyone is comfortable with public recognition, though. If that is the case, you can acknowledge their efforts privately. Private acknowledgment also allows you to be more detailed and focused, drilling down on specific aspects of their contribution.

Understanding when to offer praise is essential. Here are some guidelines. Recognition is most relevant when provided regularly and shared in the moment – the earlier shared, the better. Even if you want to take time to write something up or share in a more public forum, a spontaneous comment (not on the message-board) or a high-five in the hallway, solidifies the moment. If something more official (a formal certificate or bonus) is appropriate, that can come later, but don't miss the moment to thank an employee on the spot for their hard work.

Celebrate a person's first win, especially for new hires or when they are in a new role with new challenges or responsibilities. Recognizing the first time someone gets it right is a great way to build someone's confidence.

Celebrate a team member when they've made a difference to someone else. Sometimes, it's the small things that count for a lot. It should be recognized and celebrated when employees jump in to support each other or take on a co-worker's load so the other can go on a long overdue vacation. It helps build community and lets them know those seemingly small actions make a difference and are appreciated by the whole team.

Recognize when someone's actions align with the company values, highlight when their effort or result is truly exceptional, and honor consistency in excellence and effort. Every organization runs on and is supported by quiet, ongoing, repetitive, or unglamorous tasks consistently happening in the background. Don't let those go unnoticed. Take time to appreciate people whose work is always done well but rarely celebrated. This tells them that their reliability and perseverance are not taken for granted.

You see, accomplishments don't have to be massive to be significant. When things go well, giving credit and accolades to everyone who played even the smallest part in that success is crucial. Every milestone toward achieving a successful result matters in the grand scheme of things. Make sure you include intangibles as well as tangibles. Maybe they supported other members of the team and were cheerleaders for them. That is an intangible thing that should be celebrated. Taking small-load tasks off a co-worker's plate to free up space for a special project should be recognized. Keep a running list of each of your team's (and team members') achievements, large and small.

It's also important to recognize any challenges they may have overcome to achieve results. What were the potholes that could have tripped them up on their journey? Identify the hurdles they vaulted to reach a desired benchmark. Acknowledge how it must have felt to face those setbacks, then talk about the satisfaction of bringing it all together successfully. Emphasize your team's stamina and determination. When you acknowledge the challenges each person overcame and how everything effectively fell into place, you can inspire your team to keep reaching for even more ambitious goals.

The critical key to this is that it must be authentic. There is a profound difference between acting humble as a leader and being a humble leader. Whatever result, input, or effort you're commending, make your case with genuine energy and passion, and give it a broader context that lets everyone share in it. When you consistently and genuinely recognize others' success, it solidifies a desire in them to repeat that success and generates long-term results.

The focus must be on the team rather than on you as their leader. In a group setting, always remember to acknowledge individuals by name. If a breakthrough marketing strategy was implemented, for instance, be sure to give credit to each member of the team who played a role in that strategy, at every step of the way, from idea to implementation.

Celebrating the results and success of others communicates to them that they have been seen and appreciated. They know their efforts have made a difference and will be more likely to continue in those efforts. Taking time to let your employees know their hard work is appreciated can motivate, engage, and reinforce positive behaviors and outcomes and garner trust and loyalty. Furthermore, highlighting the achievements of others helps them build a mental resume for themselves and their future leadership.

It may seem that I am saying leaders shouldn't be celebrated, but that is not the case. A leader's recognition is rarely immediate and it might not be public. Recognition for successful leadership most often comes in intangibles – with an outstanding corporate culture, high productivity, or spin-off leaders.

Guidepost

Significant leaders don't seek to receive credit, but rather seek to give credit.

ESSENTIAL #9

Work for Your Replacement

The primary objective of significant leadership is not just team accomplishment, and it's not building numbers, dollars, figures, or accolades. The true goal of leadership is building up new leaders. Your job as a leader is to replace yourself – and the more times you can do that, the better.

When Mary Kay Ash designed her cosmetics company, it very quickly became a model upon which most reputable modern-day direct sales companies are built. Mary Kay knew that if someone achieved the position of Sales Director by recruiting consultants into the company but did not encourage those recruits to become directors, that director would eventually have a unit too large to lead. More importantly, her unit would be without a leader when she retired. Mary Kay often quoted Zig Ziglar, "When you help enough people achieve what they want in life, you will achieve what you want in life." With that in mind, she established a career path that encouraged her leadership to spin off additional leaders from their units, or they could not move themselves any further up the career ladder. By consistently working to replace themselves, directors could build and grow multiple capillary leaders to share the load. They moved ahead and received greater rewards, while their recruits also moved ahead and received greater rewards, and the company grew exponentially. The business model was visionary.

The principle underlying priority in significant leadership is always to replace oneself. While many believe there are natural-born leaders in the world, effective leadership isn't a skill anyone is actually born with. It's something that requires study, time, and effort to develop. Leaders are always built – by a situation, opportunity, or wise counsel. Significant leaders are constantly looking for the spark of potential in everyone they lead and encounter, mentoring leadership qualities in everyone and recognizing who is rising to the top like cream.

Knowing when someone is ready for more leadership responsibility, and offering it in metered doses, helps build confidence in emerging leaders and empowers them to take on a more substantial role going forward. Growing new leaders is an ongoing, steady process that starts with setting a good example. (Take a quick minute to look back at Essential #7 – Lead by Example.)

Let's discuss seven key components of growing new leaders.

- **Recognize their strengths.** Then work to give them opportunities to utilize those strengths for their own growth and the benefit of the team and organization. This will build their confidence while you work with them to identify a growth development plan and shore up areas that will hinder them once in leadership.

- **Give them the *right* experience.** Delegate to them, but not the toss-away tasks you don't want to do. What are the functions and skills your high-potential staff may not know but should be aware of? Delegate tasks to them that will gain them experience in those areas. Allow them to run some meetings or oversee some projects. Doing so will give them leadership experience in ensuring the team stays on task, meets the deliverables, and works collaboratively.

- **As you give them more responsibility, allow them to struggle a little bit.** When a high-potential employee comes to you with a challenge they're facing, you have choices. You can take over and resolve the issue, or you can hand them the resources they need. Both of those are viable leadership options for team members you are not preparing for leadership. But when it's a high-potential future leader, it is more beneficial to their growth to push them to figure it out independently. How would they resolve this if you weren't here? Where would they go to find the necessary resources? Of course, this doesn't mean you sit back and let someone hang out in the wind and do nothing to help them. Little by little, though, give them less assistance and more assurance that they can figure it out. Eventually, they learn how to take charge of finding what they need without your help.

- **Let them make some key decisions.** The Colonel said, "There are only two kinds of decisions, kid. Good decisions and lessons learned." Give them some critical choices to make. If they are good decisions, make sure all the praise and accolades go to them. If they are not-so-great decisions, shelter them while they process the consequences and talk through the lessons they've learned from it.

- **Help them create an ownership mentality.** You can do everything previously laid out here, coaching them on leadership consistently, day after day, but they won't utilize any of it if they don't feel like a trusted, valued, and impactful part of the team. If you teach them to make intelligent, informed decisions but still require them to pass every idea by you before they make a move, how empowered have you really made them? Creating an ownership mentality starts with trust. Trust them to come up with ideas, make decisions, and plan strategies. Then, empower them with authority to implement those strategies. This also requires listening to their ideas for the overall team and implementing those ideas when they make sense. When you empower your high-potentials to feel like they are an integral part of the company's future, they will more easily rise to the occasion and step into leadership.

- **Help them battle imposter syndrome.** Everyone suffers from the imposter syndrome demon now and again. If you say you don't, you either need a healthy dose of humility, are lying, or are in denial. I have been training and mentoring leaders for nearly 25 years and still struggle with it periodically. As your high-potentials grow into their leadership positions, there will invariably be a need to build and support their self-confidence and self-assurance. Everyone sometimes doubts themselves – men, women, older, younger, more experienced, and junior workers. Take the time to highlight the value they bring to the team and the company. Give them clear and consistent feedback on what they've done well with those they lead and how they can improve their team leadership. Focus on their successes first and how to bring that same energy to areas that are not going so well. Building confidence is a consistent, continuous discussion that requires recognition and reinforcement – and then some more recognition and reinforcement.

This allows you to slowly transition from boss to mentor as you help them plan their future. None of this growth will matter if they can't actually see their potential in leadership, with your organization or any other. Go from being a supervisor to an advisor. Find opportunities to meet with your high-potential employees one-on-one to ask them about their goals. What ideas might they want to implement once they are leading a team? What do they think their primary challenges will be? Help them create a purpose, mission, and vision for themselves and a plan for getting there.

It is important to note that seeing when someone is not quite ready for more responsibility is equally crucial. Being given leadership responsibility too soon can undermine someone's confidence and prevent them from believing in themselves when the time is right. In that situation, significant leaders take the opportunity to spend more time and keep a firmer (metaphorical) hand on the pupil until they are better prepared.

As leaders, it's our job to give each member of our team the opportunity and resources to grow into their own leadership style. Some will rise to the challenge and others will not, but all should be given a chance. Your reputation as a leader will grow in proportion to the number and quality of new leaders who rise with you.

Guidepost

Guiding and building up new significant leaders is the single most important duty of a leader.

PART III

Going Forward into the Future

Why Good People Stay – Living the Nine Essentials

One of my favorite long-term clients is on the leadership team of a consumer technology company. We will call him Ken and the company, WidgetTech. (True story, though names and company details are altered slightly to maintain client confidentiality.) The community culture at WidgetTech is quite astounding. There is a cohesion throughout the entire organization that starts with the company values.

Company values define how an organization lives the purpose of the business. More than just being a lofty corporate ideal, everything we do should be fueled by and predicated on the company values. WidgetTech has truly clear and well-defined core values. When the company's "Core Four" were revised in 2018, they were not only rolled out in all-branded literature but woven into the very fabric of the way the company does business, as well as how it communicates with and treats its employees and customers. These "Core Four" are articulated in a simple and easy-to-remember anagram that employees from the C-Suite to building maintenance can repeat spontaneously. Because of this, the question, "Does it honor the Core Four?" is at the center of every decision made within the company.

Across the company, leadership listens and responds to employees, engages with them, and supports their needs and dreams. Employees, especially those of younger generations, can balance their sense of purpose with paying their bills and professional growth. Indeed, the entire organization is an excellent example of what corporate culture can look like when leaders habitually practice the Nine Essentials. Let's take a look at how this manifests itself throughout the company.

Understand Your Own Value

While humbly understanding your own value is perhaps the most challenging leadership essential to measure, the existence of this first and primary essential is crucial to the remaining eight. It would be difficult to look at an organization from the outside and say with certainty that its leaders demonstrate healthy self-esteem; however, I can confidently say that WidgetTech's company culture would not be possible if arrogance and a lack of self-esteem characterized its leadership. Understanding your own value *must* come first, paving the way for the other traits of significant leaders.

Treat All People With Respect

WidgetTech employees are treated with an attitude of transparency and respect. They know where they stand and where the company is headed. WidgetTech leaders are visible and accessible, with very few barriers to communication up and down the ladder. The employees know their questions will be answered honestly, with no hedging. They trust their leadership to refrain from making promises they don't intend to honor or have no power to implement. When difficult circumstances arise, leadership is honest about the next steps and solutions, even if those aren't going to be easy.

There is a company-wide commitment to embrace diversity in all its forms – diversity in hiring, diversity in the total human, in thought, and in approaches. Welcoming diversity allows a greater sense of inclusion and belonging that goes beyond just policies and employee resource groups and is genuinely reflected in how teams and employees interact daily.

Employees are encouraged to be their authentic selves at work, which creates a sense of safety, physically, intellectually, and emotionally. This sense of security allows team members to express a differing opinion or new idea without fear, even when managers and senior leaders might disagree. There is rarely any paralyzing fear of being fired for making a mistake. It's understood that mistakes lead to growth and are used as learning opportunities. This freedom from fear increases innovation, productivity, and commitment.

Employees aren't worried when their colleagues excel at a given task or project because there's no manufactured competition, playing one team member against another. In fact, team members often discuss their duties and try to help each other find solutions. It gives them energy, and they are constantly working together to brainstorm ways to get it done or make it better. When the outcome exceeds expectations, they encourage and congratulate each other without animosity. A genuine sense of community creates friendships and a support structure beyond standard working hours.

The front-and-center availability of leadership and this organizational commitment to respect creates a sense that "we're all in this together," which makes the employees more devoted to working toward the company's mission.

Act With Integrity At All Times

Everyone places a high emotional value on integrity and a perception of "fairness." Because of the company's commitment to the "Core Four," WidgetTech employees believe they all have a fair opportunity to succeed. Surprisingly, fair pay isn't the primary factor in WidgetTech's overall employee satisfaction. Other, less tangible factors, such as faith in leadership's commitment to the workforce and a belief that employees are seen for who they are as individuals, play a much larger role.

This sense of fairness engenders trust – which is crucial. Employees trust their leaders to do the right thing, even when it's hard and a different choice would be easier. They trust that leadership understands that their most valuable asset is the employees and will always prioritize their well-being over productivity and profit.

Furthermore, employees feel that trust goes both ways. While it may be funny to talk about monitoring employee behaviors via hidden cameras in key locations around your building (the cafeteria and the bathrooms), and it may make for riveting reality television, it is a poor practice in real life. Indeed, the opposite is true. When you show people you consider them trustworthy, they will generally prove you right. When employees feel trusted, they are more likely to show responsibility to the company, its property, and its customers. WidgetTech trusts its employees to work flexible hours and from remote locations. This flexibility makes the workforce more dedicated because they feel trusted to meet their business goals in a manner that works for their life. The strong relationships that exist at the company generally prevent people from abusing the policy. While it is a fact of life that some measure of gossiping, backbiting, and office politics is bound to exist in any organization, WidgetTech's culture of integrity and trust tends to make this the exception, not the rule. When employees understand that they can be honest with their colleagues and trust each other, the intention behind gossiping is not necessary, and it becomes uncommon. As a standard at WidgetTech, gossiping and backbiting are not tolerated. When those behaviors do leak in, they are shut down with an encouragement to speak directly to the individual in a respectful manner. Additionally, team members often assist one another with tough conversations when that help is required, regardless of if it's a work-related problem or a personal issue.

Open Your Mind to New Possibilities

The safe environment created by the company's commitment to respect allows WidgetTech employees to open their minds to new possibilities. Tying back to the company's commitment to diversity, team members are challenged and encouraged to connect with disparate co-workers. This way, they can learn from each other and expand their understanding, which, for a software tech company, is crucial for breeding innovation. Management does not deride or suppress any new idea tossed at them. Instead, employees are encouraged to pitch even the seemingly craziest ideas, make suggestions, and think outside, beside, on top of, and under the box! The expectation is that once a new idea is out on the table, it opens everyone's mind to new possibilities. The team can grab the thought, massage it, make suggestions for improvement, and communally make it the best it can be. Not all ideas work by any means, but all are encouraged and given an initial voice. And while that supported creativity has resulted in some of the company's most popular products, it is not limited to product development. Employees are encouraged to feel comfortable offering new ideas in all divisions of the organization, from the warehouse to the call center, from facilities to human resources. This additional layer solidifies the employees' sense of ownership and loyalty to the company.

As a result of that commitment, WidgetTech employees are known for bragging about their company and encouraging their friends and neighbors to apply to work there. This means WidgetTech has a consistent pool of enthusiastic candidates to pull from when positions open up.

Craft A Vision

Working alongside the "Core Four," WidgetTech's corporate vision is a focal point for common interest, making the employees feel like they are part of something greater than themselves. The company's vision is the overarching picture of the "better tomorrow" they are all working toward, both in the short and long term. Because WidgetTech produces consumer electronics in dozens of different areas, this picture of the future is relevant to each division of the company in a unique way. Each executive communicates to their division how the vision is meaningful for them, and each director provides context for their group, and so on down the organization chart.

Understanding the corporate vision's relevance to each employee helps guide individual efforts and bring energy to the work. It allows leaders to create consistent and transparent performance standards and measurements. Articulating the vision in job postings enables candidates to self-select, based on if the company is headed in a direction they can enthusiastically support. The vision has provided context and reduced friction during the handful of times WidgetTech has needed to restructure, because employees could see how the structural changes would benefit the organization and keep it relevant in the future.

As a result of the corporate vision being so articulate and inspiring, when the founding partners retired within two years of each other, there was no ambiguity as to whether WidgetTech would continue on the path the partners had intended. There was no anxiety in the workforce because the purpose for the next two decades had been laid out, and the leadership transition was smooth with no stumbling.

Communicate Respectfully

Everyone knows communication is essential, yet it still seems to be a primary shortfall in most organizations – especially in the hybrid reality of a post-pandemic world. That is why WidgetTech makes it a priority. There is no such thing as too much communication in the company. Because of that, there's very little sense of "silos" between the various divisions and teams. Everyone knows that effective communication benefits everybody across the organization, so information is shared freely when available and there are few secrets or hidden agendas. Staff is rarely surprised by news that hasn't been discussed in team meetings because new talking points are communicated effectively well in advance of when the information will affect individuals.

Leaders consistently ask workers open-ended questions about both product development and their working environment. Then they respectfully and empathetically listen to the responses – even when the reactions are not favorable. This gives the company's leadership critical insight into potential corporate potholes before they show up, and it allows them to improve proactively.

Because teams are cross-communicating consistently and respectfully, deadlines are very rarely missed. When a build or feature falls behind, it's communicated to every other team that might be affected, which allows them to plan and offer suggestions on how to bring it in on time. Plus, because the communication standard is productive and respectful, recommendations are usually appreciated.

While conflict is inevitable any time human beings spend a concentrated amount of time together, a culture of considerate communication helps limit both the instance and severity of the conflict. Individuals are encouraged and empowered to express their differences respectfully, preserving the working relationship and recognizing the value of each person's input and presence. Disrespectful language, intimidation, or bullying are causes for immediate censure and potential termination if they're recurring.

Lead by Example

WidgetTech leadership is intentional about setting an example in several key areas. The first is excellence. Employees are challenged and inspired to be their best at all times, whether it's writing a new feature for a product, interacting with a customer at the call center, keeping the facilities maintained or preparing tasty meals for the cafeteria – the atmosphere of excellence motivates people to see greatness in themselves and each other.

WidgetTech leaders are diligent in their personal adherence to company policies, whether it's working hours, paid time off, use of company equipment, expense billing, or company credit cards.

This sets a standard for everyone else to follow. As a result, there is a minuscule amount of policy abuse or fraud within the workforce. This frees up the Human Resource Department's time to focus on benefitting the employees, because they don't have to be the policy police.

Leadership sets an example for positivity, community, and smiles. They intentionally smile at people they meet in the hallways and stop to greet them, asking about their day or their weekend. This challenges individuals to do the same with each other. The feeling of community at WidgetTech is palpable and often referred to as "family." Leaders at all levels of the organization work to learn at least a little about each direct report, their families, lives, joys, and struggles. This provides them with a foundation for connection, compassion, and empathy. During the height of the pandemic, executive-level leaders consistently sent out personalized, motivational messages to every employee, letting them know the company had their back and they would all get through it together.

A vital aspect of the company's vision is giving back to the community that has supported them in its explosive growth. WidgetTech leaders set the example for that as well. When the employees see their executives participating in charity runs, hosting food or coat drives, and organizing teams to volunteer at the local food bank or to help build shelters for the homeless, they are also motivated to get involved. This team spirit outside the office strengthens the company name in the community and the camaraderie in the workplace.

Celebrate The Results Of Others
The WidgetTech C-Suite regularly searches for individuals to recognize for their achievements. They are assisted by leaders in every division

who intentionally look for things that can be celebrated and shared with the "higher ups." They consistently "report up" on what their teams are doing well. This helps individuals see how much the company values their contributions and recognizes how they benefit the team and the company's overall vision. This process has also created an environment where team members brag about each other to the leader or directly to the C-Suite, which further strengthens the team and the sense of community in the organization.

It's important to note that this recognition is not limited to company success or achievements. When one employee's son competed in the Winter Olympics, WidgetTech opened the cafeteria during off-hours and hosted a watch party so everyone could see him compete live and not on broadcast delay. He didn't win a medal, but that didn't matter because everyone who wanted to be was there cheering him together. After the Olympics were over that year, WidgetTech hosted a recognition ceremony for all the Olympians from the metropolitan area.

This commitment to celebrating others further strengthens the employees' loyalty and enthusiasm to encourage others to apply and work there. Indeed, the company consistently rates 4.5–5 stars on the Glassdoor ranking website.

Work For Your Replacement

That brings us back to my client, Ken. Ken is a quiet and significant leader, a student of human nature, an avid reader, and a generally pleasant guy. Starting at entry level in his organization with an associate degree and an exceptional work ethic, he worked his way consistently through the ranks. I started mentoring him when he became the first team leader in his department. From there, his responsibilities grew, as did the amount of trust afforded him by his boss.

During one of our monthly calls, Ken communicated that he was really struggling.

"Talk to me," I said. "What's the problem? Let's figure it out."

"The problem," he responded, "is the explosive growth the company has experienced in the past three years. I mean, growth is great. That's what every company wants. But it's kind of a double-edged sword. The great side is the increased revenue and opportunities. The downside of this growth is that my department has expanded to the point where I am really struggling to manage it. I feel like it's getting out of my control."

"Some might say growth is a good problem to have," I said, "although I can see how it can create issues. What do you think the answer to this challenge is?"

"Can I clone myself?"

"Not sure that's legal. But there might be a different way to look at the same solution…"

I let that hang in the air long enough for him to realize that he didn't need to do it all himself. (In fact, leaders who try to do it all themselves eventually lose their effectiveness altogether.)

"I need to build new managers," he finally said.

"How many?"

"Oh . . . half a dozen?"

"You can do that, Ken. I think it's a good plan. It's not going to be easy. You will have to shift your paradigm and change how you lead, but I know you can do it. I'll be here to back you up on that paradigm shift."

That was all the encouragement Ken needed. He got to work training the highest-potential, top performers in his department to take on team leadership roles. He started shifting his focus from directing the work to guiding those who are directing the work. He drilled down on the Nine Essentials, first filtering his efforts through essential number nine. Some of the things he tried worked really well. Some didn't. Some of his efforts paid off immediately, while some took more time. But over the next year and a half, Ken not only met his goal, but tripled it, growing eighteen of his team members to team leadership positions, and his efforts are now focused on mentoring his leadership team.

Ken's reputation as a leader-mentor grew, and his role in the company grew. He is now the Director of Quality Assurance for the entire division.

Another unexpected byproduct emerged from Ken's efforts. Interestingly, Ken is best known for the workers who leave his division. While that may seem like an unfortunate thing to be known for, in Ken's case it isn't. This is because Quality Assurance has become a breeding ground for future leaders in the company. Over the past decade, an average of 70 percent of the engineers in his division have been promoted to leadership positions within the company. That's the kind of revolving door you want to have!

What makes Ken's team of leaders so unique? And why are there so many prospects from all areas of the company clamoring to get into his division, even at entry level? The answer can be found in the manner in which Ken leads. Simply put, he is intentionally committed to helping others grow.

While Ken's division has an outstanding record of growing leaders that continue to serve the company, he would not have been able to achieve that without the support of the company culture. WidgetTech as a whole has a specific commitment to building leaders from the inside. Every new hire is told from their first day that the ceiling is open for them. If they want to grow in their career, WidgetTech wants them to stay and grow with this company. Part of the self-evaluations that Ken and other leaders submit every year is a section on developing leaders. They answer questions like, "What am I doing to help make each member of my team better personally and professionally?"; "What have I done this year to help each person in my charge achieve their career growth goals?"; and, "Who have I mentored toward leadership this year and how?"

WidgetTech also puts its money where its mouth is regarding leadership development. The company pays employees for college courses to further their career and leadership growth. They can participate in online classes, in-person courses on-site, webinars, and individual coaching with outside consultants.

This corporate commitment to grow their future leaders from within provides WidgetTech with some key benefits. Firstly, as individual contributors become supervisors, leaders, directors, and executives, their knowledge of and commitment to WidgetTech's values, vision, and community environment are strengthened. The WidgetTech employees are not faced with outsiders stepping into executive positions and wanting to change things immediately. It provides stability and security to the workforce. Secondly, in a world where tech firms are averaging 23–45 percent annual attrition[4], WidgetTech is averaging 6.7 percent yearly attrition. I sincerely believe that is because there's truly an opportunity for growth for every employee and a fierce commitment to protecting the company's extraordinary corporate culture.

A Final Thought

Imagine having a workforce that wakes up every day enthusiastic about going to work. Imagine employees who get along with little to no drama and collaborate to improve each other, their product, and their company. If this is not your current reality, that's okay. We all have to start somewhere. Leadership is a noble endeavor that is rarely easy but always fulfilling.

A saying often attributed to being an "ancient Chinese proverb" says, "The hardest part of any journey is the first step. Once you get that out of the way, you'll find the rest of the journey much easier." That is not entirely the case here, because significant leadership requires daily dedication, and there is never a downhill slope upon which to coast. But I am confident that you must commit and take that first step toward significant leadership to truly be the leader you were intended to be. You deserve to be a significant leader, and those you lead deserve a significant leader guiding them. The first step every day is to commit to focusing all your leadership efforts through the lens of The Nine Essentials of Significant Leadership. If you are new to leadership, it's essential to understand that the skills that got you noted and promoted are different from those that will make you a significant leader. Significant leadership requires a shift in focus, transitioning from one who manages the work to one who leads those who are doing (or managing) the work.

Let the Nine Essentials be a guide for that transition. Solidify your belief in your own value as a human being and the value you bring to the table as a leader. Endeavor to treat all people with respect whether or not you like what they think, say, or do. Do what is right every time, whether anyone is looking or not. Open your mind to see every situation from all sides, and contemplate new possibilities. Visualize the best future for each member of your team. Communicate respectfully and in a manner that makes it easy for the listener to absorb and act upon. Set an example of what you would expect to see from each person you lead or encounter. Set aside your need to be recognized and find ways to recognize those around you. Help others grow into leadership.

If you are a seasoned leader, you need to understand that while the 20th-century hierarchal mentality of employee-as-replaceable-commodity (for the purpose of making a higher profit for the stakeholders) leaked into the first twenty years of this century, it is no longer a viable working model. Our current fragile situation and the differing priorities of a majority-millennial workforce prove that if you want to survive and thrive going forward, there must be a shift in focus and priorities. Let the Nine Essentials be a guide for that paradigm shift.

Avoiding the revolving door of attrition and attracting and retaining great employees is not simply about providing more money, great benefits, or great "perks." While free doughnuts, salty snacks, and coffee and soda all day long may be a nice idea (one that will probably add to your employees' weight and blood pressure!), it will not come close to keeping an employee who is considering looking elsewhere. And though the concepts in this book may seem very high-level and less practical, my research and experience have proven to me that the critical bottom-line factors of reduced attrition, increased productivity, customer satisfaction, market share, and profitability will all fall into place when you put a stronger emphasis on the Nine Essentials of Significant Leadership.

Building an environment that sustains a 10 percent (or lower) attrition rate requires working diligently to craft a culture wherein employees trust their leaders from the top down, take pride in the excellence of their work, and enjoy the people they work with, treating them with respect. A corporate environment of enthusiasm, productivity, performance, trust, and loyalty requires significant leadership at every company level.

What would happen if you committed to using the Nine Essentials in your everyday actions as a leader? Make it a daily discipline. Discipline becomes habits, and habits become character traits. Start with one step, one day. Then, keep that focus for one week, then one month, then six months, then a year. If you could reduce your attrition and increase your productivity, profitability, employee engagement, and loyalty by just making that one commitment, how would that change your company? I think it's worth a shot.

I can't wait to hear what *your* results are.

Acknowledgments

All praise, honor, and glory to my Father in Heaven, who is bigger, stronger, wiser, and more patient even than I could ever hope or expect and who crafted me for a specific purpose.

Thank you to the love of my life, my husband, and my best friend, Ron Schieffer. You always believe that I am more intelligent and more gifted than I think I am. I am continually amazed and inspired by how hard you work at being a significant leader. I wouldn't want to do life with anyone else.

Thank you to Mark LeBlanc, who helped me visualize The Nine Essentials of Significant Leadership and is the best combination of friend and business coach anyone could ask for.

Thank you to Henry DeVries for your formatting and layout recommendations that allowed me to see the book before I wrote it.

Profound gratitude to the significant leaders I have had the privilege to know, follow and learn from: My father – LtCol Gerald G Leigh, Sen John McCain, Gen Colin Powell, Mary Kay Ash, Dr. John C. Maxwell, Barry Banther, Dr. Nido Quibein, Steven Iwersen, and countless others along my journey.

About the Author

Lauren Schieffer's passion is helping organizations build their next generation of leaders. Whether it's training, keynotes or longer-term consulting partnerships, Lauren uses her *Nine Essentials of Significant Leadership* to help transform the way managers think, make decisions, and act toward the people they lead.

Organizations bring Lauren on because she brings a fresh new perspective and a street-smart approach to what works and what doesn't. She helps speed transformation in three critical areas: knowledge, skills and relationships.

She provides your people with what they need to know to be better leaders, helps them develop the skills critical to their success and their influence, and shows them ways to build stronger relationships with the people they serve and lead.

As a result, your people will be more focused on what matters every day. They'll lead with compassion and integrity, and they'll create and model standards of excellence that others will aspire to and follow – all centered behind a common goal and vision.

That's what significant leadership is.

Can Hiring Lauren Benefit You?

When you need someone with a proven track record of building emerging leaders past efficiency and servant, into significant leadership, Lauren is the natural choice.

When you are ready to dump the drama and improve the effectiveness of your leadership and communication, Lauren can help.

Whether you are looking for an exceptional, motivating keynote, on-going training, consulting, retreat facilitation, mastermind groups or one-on-one coaching, Lauren is the one to call.

Reach out today. You'll be so thankful you did.

www.**LaurenSchieffer**.com
Lauren@LaurenSchieffer.com
913-530-6673

Works Cited

[1] Teevan, J., Baym, N., Butler, J., Hecht, B., Jaffe, S., Nowak, K., Sellen, A., and Yang, L. (Eds.). Microsoft New Future of Work Report 2022. Microsoft Research Tech Report MSR-TR-2022-3 (https://aka.ms/nfw2022), 2022

[2] Meister, J. Employees Weigh In On What's Important to Them and Why They Stay at Their Companies. (https://www.paychex.com/articles/human-resources/employee-retention-what-makes-employees-stay-leave), 7/28/2022

[3] Microsoft Report. Technology Can Help Unlock a New Future For Frontline Workers. https://www.microsoft.com/en-us/worklab/work-trend-index/technology-unlocks-a-new-future-for-frontline, Trend Index Special Report Survey conducted on behalf of Microsoft by research firm, Edelman Data x Intelligence.

[4] Bendor-Samuel, P. Spiking Attrition Impact on IT and Engineering Services. https://www.forbes.com/sites/peterbendorsamuel/2022/05/31/spiking-attrition-impact-on-it-and-engineering-services/?sh=73c7b26f7c99, 5/31/2022

Made in the USA
Monee, IL
07 June 2023